THE
OUTSIDERS

MARGARET
SMITH

CHRISTIAN FOCUS PUBLICATIONS

© 1991 Margaret Smith
ISBN 1 871676 525

Published by
Christian Focus Publications Ltd
Geanies House, Fearn IV20 1TW
Ross-shire, Scotland, UK.

Printed and bound in Great Britain
by Cox & Wyman Ltd, Reading

Cover illustration
by
Mike Taylor

Cover design
by
Seoris McGillivray

CONTENTS

In memory
of my parents

John and Johanna Smith

1
SAND, SEAWEED AND SARCASM

Glancing behind her, she saw him break into a run and head towards her. With a pounding heart, fighting fear and rising panic, Donna ran - picking up speed with every step. What would happen if he caught her?

Choking back tears, Donna sent up a quick prayer. "Please God, if you're there, help me - please?" But her prayer felt like a cowardly act, that of a little girl running to God in time of danger, and forgetting him otherwise. Yet, her guilty conscience pricked her only for a moment as she gasped for breath and ran on. She left the village behind and neared the shore - and Stewart Steele was now only yards behind her and quickly gaining on her! Her feet lost their grip as she struggled on, and in the moments that followed, Donna slipped down the shingle slope, with nothing to grasp, as the stones hurtled down at equal speed. When she did at last stop, she was surrounded by stones, shingle, sand and sea-weed.

Above her now towered Stewart Steele, smiling his hard little smile and asking in feigned concern, "Are you all right? You're not hurt, are you?"

She knew he didn't care. Physically, Donna was unscathed but - yes - she was hurt! Her pride had taken a heavy blow. After one shocked and defeated moment, she stood and faced him squarely.

"What do you want anyway? Were you following me?" she asked, as she brushed the sand off her jeans.

"Don't flatter yourself, Donna." His face contorted with contempt more than anger. "I just saw you and decided to sort you out, once and for all. But don't worry, I wouldn't touch you with a barge-pole!"

She met his cold stare and saw that this was serious business. Stewart's eyes, usually an uncertain grey, were now black-stormy, and the jaw was square, accentuating his high cheek bones. Eyebrows met in the middle and the lips tightened into one angry thin line. Donna forced herself to return his stare and fumbled to produce her usual approach line.

"My mother will be really mad when I tell her. She'll see about you. Just you wait and see, Stewart Steele. You won't get off with this!" The words were those of a primary-school child, which she recognised, but was powerless to change. As she expected, he returned her threats in his usual sneering, sarcastic manner.

"Aw, tell your mum to kick-start her broomstick and... No, go on, run to mammy. Seventeen years old and still a skirt hider-behind! You're just a snob - you *and* your mam, living up there in your posh kit-built mansion, and passing judgment on everything and everyone. Just *who* do you think you are - huh?"

Donna opened her mouth to deny all, but no opportunity was given.

"You and your mother are behind all those rumours about me being a thief - right?"

"Wrong!" she hissed.

Once he started though, the words cascaded like an angry torrent of water. "It's true!" he continued, "things go missing, then guess what - me, the East End guy from Glasgow gets called a thief!"

Anger, rising within her at alarming speed, forced Donna to let emotions spill over into her own personal tirade against this boy who so often made her snarl inside.

"We're not the only ones who think that, you know. Things *never* went missing here - at least not before you came last winter," she yelled, throwing caution to the winds.

"Ever heard of coincidence," Stewart threw back. "It does happen, you know - even on this 'Holy Isle'. It might suit you to conveniently blame the incomer, but just get this straight - I don't go in for that kind of thing. It's just not my style."

Flinging all her strength into her words Donna spat out, "Oh, just push off, Stewart! Why don't you just go right back to wherever you came from and leave me alone!"

"Yeah, go back to high rise flats, graffiti, damp walls and late night street fights - you'd like that, Donna."

"Sure I would! Anything to get you out of my life," she answered in a fury of irritation, although his words made her realize that she had no conception of his previous lifestyle or circumstances. She had no yardstick by which to judge them. Yet, unwilling to let him see any softening of her attitude, she turned quickly to go, but Stewart grabbed her roughly by the arm.

"Not so fast, you spoilt brat!"

"Hey, boys aren't supposed to ill-treat girls." She lightened her tone, aiming for nonchalance. "It's bad for their image."

"Don't push your luck," he snapped, but he let go of her arm. His face was tight with anger, two bony knobs in his jaw working as he spoke. "You know I came to this island as a total stranger. 'You won't be a stranger in the Western Isles for long,' I kept being told. 'The folk are so kind and friendly.' Well, Donna, that's some joke, isn't it!"

"Stewart, it's your own fault," she responded. "Just look at you - all noise and leather - and worst of all, that gold cross earring. You know that it offends the church-goers in these parts. You're just asking for trouble - that's you're problem, pal!"

"You're dead right there, Donna!" That's exactly why I wear it. See, I *did* go to church on my very first Sunday here - just to please Aunt Rachel. Next day, and guess what, some old guy's moaning to her because I had no tie on. Well, that kind of attitude will change with me around. I'll show you; your little-village mentality is in for a big surprise!"

With that, he turned abruptly on his heel and strode away up the slope with long, elastic steps, sending down a new rush of slithering stones. Soon he was out of sight altogether and moments later the faint sound of his motorbike signalled his leaving.

Donna sat on a nearby boulder and felt her anger dying - it was too energetic an emotion to sustain for long. Her flushed cheeks cooled in the stiff on-coming breeze, and her heartbeat slowed down to its usual steady rhythm. Raising her head, she looked out to sea. The huge waves crashed in on the shore, sending sheets of spray in all directions. Sifting soft sand through her fingers, Donna kicked the pebbles at her feet as if to give a final outlet to any remaining fury. Then she sat, silent and motionless, hands, once quivering, now stuffed in the pockets of her denim jacket.

But her thoughts were racing. She tried to take in all that had happened in the storminess of those past moments. Donna had to admit to herself that she was not used to being anything else other than loved and admired. She was an only child; loved and wanted from birth to the present day. Her father, a seaman, brought her gifts from all corners of the globe, and doted on her in the months they spent together when he was at home on leave each year. Her mother treated Donna like a young sister and enjoyed their relationship, being constantly ambitious for her only daughter.

Friends? Well, Donna had one good friend, Mairi Martin from the next village - and there were plenty of others. Donna sometimes wondered if they would bother if she wasn't so well off! Quite often these friends used her make-up, read her books and magazines and borrowed her clothes. She liked them though, and they enjoyed each other's company. Smiling, she thought of their good times together. Yes - Donna concluded, she *was* popular, well liked, well-off.

Pride at her own status changed quickly to revenge on Stewart Steele for his attitude to her and his actions towards her. "I'll show you, Stewart. Nobody treats me like this and gets away with it - nobody!"

Anger, a feeling of dejection, a thirst for revenge, a devilment rising up inside her - all those feelings fluttered in her mind like birds, none willing to settle. Standing up steadily, she looked at the spit and roar of the sea, and the majesty of the ancient cliffs jutting out here and there along the bleak and lonely coastline.

Seagulls circled above, wheeling, diving, constantly moving. Their screams echoed and re-echoed above the crashing of the ceaseless waves. In the sea, a grey seal surfaced, glossy in the autumn light. Despite the cool breeze and the raging sea, the dying sun had laid a red-and-gold path over the expanse before her, almost adding warmth to the waves.

Yet its soothing quality left her untouched, and Donna felt only the cold bitterness of a new desperate search for revenge rising in her heart, overshadowing everything within her and around her. Pulling her jacket collar up around her neck, she turned around and headed for home with that last thought churning over constantly in her mind. Revenge above all else. Yes, she would take that whiz-kid Glaswegian down a peg or two!

"I'll show him - I'll show you, Stewart Steele. You won't get away with it! Just you wait and see!"

2
TEA AND SYMPATHY

On reaching the safety of home, Donna launched into an angry narrative of her meeting with Stewart Steele.

"He did what! Where did this happen? Did he hurt you?" Her mother's reaction was a welcome relief and Donna enjoyed giving all the details, whilst anticipating each new wave of anger come rushing to her mother's whole being. Mrs Macdonald stood there, at times fiddling nervously with her perfectly styled auburn hair, and at other times taking her anger out on the peats as she bent to arrange them and re-arrange them on the open fire.

"He hates me like poison, mum. I know he does and - well - I'm not exactly crazy about him either! He should never have come here. He just doesn't fit in." Donna summed up aloud all her thoughts, and Mrs Macdonald's approving nod suggested an instant agreement with Donna's last statement.

Drawing the soft, grey velvet curtains together, Donna paused momentarily to admire the beautiful September harvest moon. Tonight it was big and butter-gold, so full it seemed too heavy for the sky to hold. In Gaelic, it was called *gealach bhuidhe an Fhogair* - the 'golden autumn moon.' It poured down its warm, wonderful glow, catching the pine trees in its half-light, throwing shadows on the

square lawn and on the sleeping September flowers. Oh
- to frame that picture in the mind, Donna thought. She
wished she was artistic and able to take that scene and
reproduce it in beautiful autumn colours on canvas, forever to be remembered and admired. Turning away she
caught her mother's words.

"I think it's time I spoke to the authorities about that
boy! After all, how can that aunt of his, well - his great-aunt
- how can she look after him in her old age? A boy with
that unmanageable amount of energy. And she's not
well."

"I wouldn't be well either if I had *him* in my house,"
Donna commented. "But mum, what can you do about it?"

Mrs Macdonald's frown changed into a rather brittle
smile as she replied dryly, "Oh Donna, I know a few
people who could pull quite a few strings! That boy would
be much better off right back where he came from, and
we'd be glad to see the back of him! He'd get on better
- fit in better in Glasgow with his own kind of people. His
poor great-aunt shouldn't have that kind of thing in her
life, she's so old and frail. How can *she* tame or change
his wild Glasgow ways?"

To Donna, her mother's speech was balm and she
hoped any other future audience would feel as responsive
as she felt. Obviously her mother too was quite ready to
pack Stewart Steele off on the very next ferry sailing! As
a result, Donna cheered up instantly and offered to make
a refreshing cup of tea.

"Not for me dear. I'll take a can of coke instead."
Donna ambled through to the kitchen and moved the
kettle back on to the hottest part of the stove. The stove,
packed with peat, soon had the kettle singing and bub-

bling as it sent out a cloud of steam. Meanwhile Donna had popped one of Granny's floury scones into the microwave and now it waited on her sideplate, topped with a very generous helping of 'crowdie and cream'. Well, why not! Nothing could beat Granny's home baking and after all, Donna definitely needed cheering.

As she handed her mum the can of coke she thought it curious that her mum - a real 'tea-jenny' - had in recent months left the teapot untouched, while at the same time she seemed to be putting away coke by the gallon. As she watched her, it came to her also that her mother seemed increasingly tired and washed out lately. Her evenings seemed to be spent lying on the couch. Warning bells were ringing, but Donna couldn't wrench the meaning out of them although she probed deeply within herself.

Now her mother laid aside the homework she was correcting and wearily stretched out, trying to rub the sleep from her eyes. Being a schoolteacher was her first love and Donna knew it brought fulfilment to her mother's life as she taught those little ones all she could. Yet tonight, Donna thought her mother looked weary of it all, as if something much more was happening in her personal life. What was it?

"I'm whacked, love!" her mother said as she sipped her coke and watched it run around the rim. "I think a slow bath and a quiet read in bed before sleeping should help me relax."

It seemed a real opportunity for Donna to quiz her mother. "Mum, are you all right? You seem so stressed-out lately and just not your usual self. You're off your food and here you are - sipping coke!" Even as she blurted out her personal findings, the swift fear that gripped her increased as she thought of what her mother's answer might be. What if she were ill? How could she cope without her mum around?

Mrs Macdonald kept her eyes on the rim of her coke tin and then almost awkwardly, she lifted her gaze to meet Donna's questioning look. "Well, Donna, it's time we told you." She paused there and took a deep breath. "I'm expecting a baby - in February."

For a long moment, Donna just kept staring, whilst the words drifted over to her and lodged in her brain. As she grappled for words, her mind became a woolly blank, every thought out of joint, miles apart.

"Well dear, are you pleased? Go on, say you're shocked! After all, you're seventeen and the only one. I'm forty now and nearly too old for babies. We...we thought you'd be really happy once you get used to the idea!" Mrs Macdonald's racy tones and flickering eyelids indicated her own tension at that moment, as she glanced nervously from coke tin to daughter in the hope of an eventual positive reaction.

Meanwhile, realization had trickled through Donna's mind. The pieces of the puzzle had come together. A baby! A new brother or sister! After all this time! What could she say?

"Come on, Donna, don't keep me on edge - what do you think?" her mum repeated with a smile that definitely quivered around the edges.

Finally, "Oh...um...yes. That's brilliant, mum. Of course I'm pleased."

Donna's effort at sounding positive wouldn't have won her an Oscar, but eager to press on, her mother launched into the inevitable Phase Two of the conversation. "Would you prefer a brother or a sister?" she asked, now putting down her coke tin and relaxing a little.

"Oh, I don't mind really," Donna replied, almost too quickly. "Well, perhaps a wee brother. I've always wanted a brother." She knew it was a lie. She liked being an only child. Yet, racking her brains for something useful to say, she came up with the next obvious question. "Have you thought of a name yet?"

Mrs Macdonald, relaxing fully into the conversation, smiled at her daughter's obvious delight and involvement. "Oh yes, dear. We've come up with a few; Morna or Roma for a girl, and Calvin or Kelvin for a boy. What do you think?

Donna thought the names sounded pretty awful - straight out of an American soap-opera. However, once again she found a lie coming too readily to her lips. "Mmmm, lovely. Very modern."

And so the conversation meandered around the big event. Would mother leave work? Would the baby mean less money? The answer to both were 'yes' - but with an unexpected spin-off. Donna would have to forego her driving lessons till later.

"You're not too disappointed about that, dear?"

"No way! I didn't mind cruising up and down our drive, but remember when Daddy took me out on the side road?"

"How could I forget!" her mother laughed. "A sheep ran out in front of the car."

"And I screamed, opened the door and jumped out of the car. Dad was hopping mad. He had to do some weird and wonderful acrobatics to get into the driver's seat!"

"And that put an end to your driving ambition!"

Despite the humorous asides, it was drastic, unthinkable news for Donna. Her robotic 'question-and-answer' routine had been a camouflage to hide the real emotional impact of her mother's news. To Mrs Macdonald, the hard part of 'telling' was over and now had her daughter's self sacrificing love and support to see her through thick and thin. Both smiled at each other, but each smile, for Donna, concealed the confused thoughts squirrelling within her mind.

When a suitable moment came, Donna made her exit. To Mrs Macdonald, it was the usual 'goodnight mum' and a kiss on the forehead - but how very wrong she was to suppose that all was well.

For, once within the safety of her own bedroom, that wide and supple smile vanished, the laughter ceased and the 'real' Donna expressed herself fully. She steadied herself by glaring at her image in the full length wall mirror. The long, thick, glossy-brown hair was tossed back in anger. The colour in her cheeks faded to a pale, and her ready smile was replaced by a glower that made her look as bad as she felt.

She took several deep breaths, repeating on each exhalation, "It's okay. It's okay." And then, "You can handle this - no problem. Please God, don't let this happen to me!" Again it came to her how she only called on God when she was in a corner. And her stricken conscience only added to her misery.

Once in bed, she snuggled for warmth under the covers, playing each scene over and over in her mind. A brother - a sister - coming to spoil the loveliness of her little world. Now her parents' time and attention would be split between her and this - this other person.

It was not a comfortable thought, nor was her earlier episode with Stewart Steele. Both together, churning over in her mind, left Donna tossing and turning well into the wee small hours.

Finally exhausted, and with her mind now permanently stuck in the same groove, Donna felt sleep overtake her and she drifted off into a world of wild and restless dreams.

3
BABY TALK AND A MISSING CALCULATOR

One week later found Donna sitting with her friends at school, making a little cluster of conversation. It was a lazy, warm September morning and the sun shone brightly through the huge classroom windows. The desks smelt of that warm sticky smell, peculiar to school furniture. Outside on a window ledge, there was a mad little bird nearly bursting his throat with the joy of living. Inside, Donna felt less than eager to tell her pals about the baby, but yet she realised that putting it off indefinitely would be just as awkward.

"A baby! Yeuch, they're all noise, nappies and night time feed; yeah - dirty nappies, drools, dinner off the floor; all your clothes will stink of sour milk. They puke *all the time!* And when they get on their feet, that's when they're real nuisances - tripping over every little molecule of dust."

"Donna, you're in for one big shock! That'll be the end of life as you know it. From now on it'll be - 'he's got colic, poor thing,' 'he's teething - again - poor thing,' 'oh dear, he's missed the potty again!' "

This of course sent a raucous laugh all around. So the anti-baby tirade continued and Donna's misery at the thought was escalating in leaps and bounds.

Only Katie came to the rescue and Donna felt relieved, although she and Katie hadn't much in common. Katie was one of those 'Christians' and so moved in a totally different sphere from Donna. Yet, she liked Katie's frankness and sincerity, and listened to her personal input on the 'baby' theme.

"I think that a baby is a little miracle in its own right. A gift from God." Katie wasn't the prettiest girl in class, but when she became enthusiastic about something, her face became full of vitality. It was part of her own particular brand of charm, the kind that released itself gradually, like the perfume of a flower in the sun's warmth.

A voice prevented her from continuing. "Huh - talking of gifts - you'd need a few to afford a baby! Boy, they don't come cheap!" Then Mairi Martin added, "It's just as well your folks are well off, Donna!" Mairi's blue eyes twinkled, as she tossed back her fair hair. "They cost a fortune, what with nappies, food, clothes, baby equipment - and of course they grow so quickly you need to keep buying - just to keep up with them. Not to mention replacing what they break and tear and destroy once they get on their feet!"

"Hey, stop being so dull and pessimistic," said Katie. "Okay, babies are an expensive hobby, but they are so much more besides! And, people can always make ends meet. I mean, look at you, Mairi; both your parents are out of work just now, but you never seem to lack for anything."

At that, Mairi gently fingered her new pearl-drop earrings, before quickly changing the subject and calling to a crowd of boys who strolled into class. "Hey, how's the S.S. gang! Late as usual, I see?"

The boys were called the S.S. gang because they were the chief trouble makers and had latched onto Stewart Steele as soon as he appeared. Naturally, the boy from

Glasgow immediately became the 'leader of the pack' and had a faithful following.

"Give us a song, Katie! If you're good enough to sing for the 'God Squad', you're good enough to sing for us," sneered one, leaning back in his chair and chewing a matchstick. "You've got your guitar, haven't you?"

Their sniggering made Donna squirm. She felt uneasy, and wished he hadn't referred to the Youth Fellowship in that way.

Katie's calm, even voice brought sudden hushed silence, and Donna wondered how anyone could remain so unruffled in the middle of all that abuse. "Okay, no problem, boys. I'll sing to you - I'll sing a song describing how all of us are outside God's family until we believe in Jesus."

Someone clapped loudly as a few others laughed or shot each other sly glances. There were the usual array of sarcastic looks and quiet undefined asides. Katie began to strum gently on her 12-string guitar, her head bent low, her dark hair falling forward. As Katie sang, Donna couldn't help but listen to every word.

For ten seconds, silence reigned. Then, the classroom door was flung open. Half the class jumped clean out of their seats before quickly picking up pencils and continuing with their work. The S.S. gang, and a few other brave souls just stared, obviously waiting to enjoy the inevitable forthcoming lecture from the very irate teacher, Mr Pilkington. He was new to the school: all the way to the Western Isles from the south of England, and bringing with him all the characteristics that made him so different to the regular Hebridean. Quality English and that rather peculiar accent occupied the next few minutes.

"Pardon me! I was told to check on a Geography class. And here I stumble on a Music lesson. Kindly leave the world of entertainment and revert to reality - for example, the reality of being unemployed because you didn't make the grade!" All said, he spun round on his heel and left the classroom as abruptly as he'd entered it. The guilty carried on working while the rest promptly sat back and laughed.

Donna kept working, not because she wanted to, but because, in her mind, the words's of Katie's song ticked over and over again. What did it all mean - to be outside God's kingdom? Within her, Donna longed to know and understand, but, as usual, thoughts like that never lingered long and all too soon the shrill sound of the bell broke up Donna's train of thought.

She carried Katie's guitar for her as the class left the room, in a way hoping that Katie might say a bit more about the words of her song. Yet again, that opportunity didn't last long as Donna quickly realised that she'd left her bag in the classroom.

Handing the guitar to Mairi, she ran back towards the classroom, only to find Stewart Steele, alone, and blocking her way. "Well, well, and how's mammy's pet then?" he asked dryly as he continued to block her way.

She gave up the 'dance' and faced him squarely. "Oh, just get out of my way, and out of my life," she spat out angrily.

"Out of your life?" echoed Stewart. "Donna, I'm not even in your life - yet - but by the time I'm through with you, you'll be more miserable than you could ever imagine possible!" There was a self-confidence, almost a triumph in his voice that unnerved Donna.

"Don't bother scheming and planning to make my life a misery. Just carry on breathing."

"Nice one, Donna! You're actually quite intelligent, aren't you?"

"It's just a phase," she said airily.

"Oh, how hard you're trying to come up with smart answers! I can see that poor little brain, all twisted up like a Soviet gymnast."

"Ha, ha," she retorted, but Stewart finally stepped aside, bowed low mockingly, and let Donna past. Quickly, she grabbed her bag, left the classroom and raced along the corridor.

"At last!" Mairi said, as Donna caught up. "I was getting cheesed off with doing my I-am-a-patient-wonderful-friend routine."

"Sorry. That Steele guy hassled me. Honestly, he should have been strangled at birth!"

Mairi smiled a little. "Actually, I think he's really good-looking, don't you? Oh, come on, admit it," she said, giving Donna a sidelong glance. There was no reply from Donna, who took the guitar, gave her schoolbag to Mairi, and ran off to deposit the guitar with Katie.

Arriving five minutes late at her next class, she fumbled an apology and got stuck into her Maths exercise to make up for lost time. Frowning over an excruciatingly difficult equation, Donna reached into her bag for her calculator...but where was it? After tipping out her schoolbag it was still nowhere to be seen.

It was only then that the thought exploded like a bullet in her brain. Stewart Steele...empty classroom...missing calculator! He must have taken it - it made sense. The misery he promised had begun.

4
RACHEL'S VISIT

The calculator incident was indeed proving to be a real misery, for Donna and of course for Donna's mother. It was Wednesday evening and Donna's mum was busy preparing those last minute things for their evening meal.

Once done, they continued their conversation in the living room. "I just don't understand why the Rector didn't call the police at once," her mother began. "It's so obvious he's the guilty one, even though he's denying it."

"He would, wouldn't he!" Donna said acidly, but she squirmed at the very thought of the rector, Mr MacAulay. He made her feel so uncomfortable, almost as if *she* were the criminal. Missing calculators weren't high on his list of priorities, so that although Donna had reported the incident immediately after the Maths class, Mr MacAulay was finally only able to deal with her several days later.

Donna replayed that scene over again in her mind. Mr MacAulay was sitting behind his desk, a stocky man with iron-grey hair which was permanently dishevelled, thanks to the habit he had of running a hand through it in times of perplexity. He did it now.

"Well now, Donna, about your calculator. You know of course that Stewart Steele - whom you are openly accusing - has denied taking it. Are you quite sure it was in your schoolbag at all, Donna?" he asked, studying her over the top of his silver-rimmed spectacles.

Donna paused, to be polite and to steady her voice as frustration welled up inside her. "Yes! I mean, yes sir. I had it and I used it for my Statistics exercise - sir. I went straight from one class to the next." Having already said all of that in her first formal report Donna felt irritated at having to cover old ground again. "Perhaps, sir, if this had been dealt with earlier, you'd have a good chance of catching it on him, sir."

It was far too smart a statement for any pupil to address to a Rector and his sudden angry expression reflected that feeling. His frown drew his bushy eyebrows together into one angry line. "I hardly think so. Do you really think a thief would be that stupid? Anyway, I've done all I *can* do for the moment, Donna. I've taken details of this incident and I've informed your teachers of your suspicion. We'll keep an eye on the situation."

His dismissive brisk nod was softened by the ghost of a smile, but, for Donna it was hardly a comforting conclusion and she was still without her calculator. And surprise, surprise! - nothing at all had happened since then.

"Penny for them!" said her mother, breaking suddenly into her thoughts.

"Oh, mum - I was miles away. Thinking how nice it'll be to have a baby in the house."

Donna's mother smiled and continued along the same theme: "What do you think of this wool? Yellow's a nice colour for a new baby and I thought this matinee jacket would suit either a girl or boy."

"Mmmm, neat," Donna replied, trying hard to inject the necessary spark into her voice.

Just then, they heard the outer door open, then shut,

and footsteps quickened, then stopped at the living room door. Quietly, she entered, closing the door firmly behind her.

It was Rachel, Stewart's great-aunt. Everyone called her 'Rachel'. There was only one Rachel in the whole district and so everyone knew who Rachel was when she was ever mentioned.

"I am sorry that I just walked in," she began, and coughed apologetically. "I did knock, but nobody was coming so I just came in," she added smiling, taking off her woollen headscarf to reveal silver-white hair all caught up in a bun at the base of her neck.

"Oh - that's all right, Rachel. The television's too loud anyway," said Donna's mum, disguising her surprise by bustling around, switching off the television and bringing one of the chairs a little closer to the fire. "Have a seat, Rachel."

"Thank you, I will, but I will not be long," she replied as she warmed her thin, bony hands by the fire.

Donna found Rachel's careful 'it is' and 'I am' and 'I will' very appealing. She could have been a French woman speaking in English, for, to her, English was a foreign language. Gaelic was the language of her birth.

"You seem quite wheezy," Mrs Macdonald said conversationally. "Have you got a cold?"

"No. Well, not really, but I have been chesty like this for some months now. I have not gone to the doctor but I think I will need to go if it carries on. Stewart says I'm a stubborn old woman and will get no more sympathy from him till I do!"

The mention of Stewart had changed the atmosphere in an almost tangible way.

"It is about Stewart that I have come to see you," Rachel began, without changing the tone of her voice, but keeping a steady gaze on the peat flame. "A Social Worker came to see me some days ago. It was about a complaint, but she would not say who was the complainer - or whatever you call it. Something about Stewart chasing a girl here on the shore and frightening her. I thought it must be you Donna, because I hear that yourself and Stewart are not friendly at all."

Her simplistic language and honest approach to the situation left Donna almost speechless. "Yes - yes it was me, Rachel," she managed to croak.

"Then, I am sorry, Donna, I am sorry that he did that and that he frightened you. He should not have done it and it will not happen again."

There followed an odd silence where no-one knew quite what to say.

Eventually, Donna's mother broke in, rather briskly. "Don't you think he - Stewart's too much for you? I mean - well, is he not a handful? He's a lively thing, lots of energy - it can't be easy for you, Rachel, at your time of life."

Rachel's reply, still with warmth, was firm. "You think I am too old to cope with Stewart, don't you? Well, there is something you need to understand, Mrs Macdonald. Every day that goes past, I thank God for Stewart. Every day. You see, when you are unmarried and grow old like me, you begin to worry - 'who will look after me when I am older and unwell?' Even although I am the Lord's, I had that worry - but now I have Stewart, and, oh, if only you knew how I look forward to the sound of that school bus every afternoon! God is good, and he sent Stewart to me as an answer to my prayers."

Religious talk left Donna's mother cold and uneasy and so she quickly changed the angle of her talk. "But Rachel, surely you must agree that he would be far better back where he belongs, with his own family, in Glasgow?"

"Oh, no, not at all, Mrs Macdonald. You see, although Stewart never lacked for love or anything else, his life was a struggle and they lived in a very rough part of Glasgow."

From under slightly tufted brows her blue eyes shone with an intensity not yet dimmed by age.

"His mother - my niece - had him before she got married. Then, a few years ago, she died - she was only thirty-eight. She had meant the world to Stewart."

Rachel stopped briefly, and they sat in silence for a moment.

"Two years later," she continued, "his step-father married again but sadly, Stewart and the stepmother did not get along. His only choice was to come up here with me and make a life of his own. I know he seems a bit wild, but it would be good to remember how things have been for him. To be called a 'Glasgow hooligan' after only three weeks - well, that is not fair - to anyone."

She turned to face Donna. "He did not take your caccator - no, its cal-cu-lator, isn't it? There, I managed to say it at last! His seventeenth birthday is not long past and he got a new one of his own. He was showing me how to work it but in the end he gave up and said I must have been nowhere near the counter when brains were being handed out!"

"So you don't think..." Donna's eyes flickered with a moment of hesitation.

"No. And I am not just sticking up for him because he is my niece's son. Oh - I know about his clothes, that big noisy bike, that cross earring; yes, I speak to him about these things many times. But I always say to him too, 'Stewart, man looks on the outward appearance, God on the heart.' It is what is inside the heart that counts. If our hearts are right before God..."

"Yes, quite," Donna's mother tried to interrupt.

Rachel coughed for a few moments, then continued. "Someone once said that God has made us for himself, and that our hearts are restless until we find rest in him. That's what I tell Stewart. All the restlessness, and all the wild ways, they would soon disappear if he found Christ."

"Cup of tea?" Donna asked, sensing her mother's deepening hostility to this turn of conversation.

Mrs Macdonald could argue about politics, different religions, and so on, but when it came to a belief that was as powerful and personal as Rachel's, then she was lost for words. Donna knew from previous discussions that her mother put a strong faith like Rachel's down to lack of education, or being brainwashed by the church.

"I'll make the tea, Donna," her mother said.

She disappeared into the kitchen in a waft of perfume and the quick clippings of her heeled slippers on the tiled floor. Rachel looked at Donna with a mixture of warmth and compassion, almost as if reading her thoughts.

But all she said was, "Beautiful young lives, for God."

5
THE TRUTH DISCOVERED

In the weeks that followed, Donna tried to forget Rachel's words. In her mind, however, those eyes, still and wise and old, continued to look at her with compassion.

Along with most of her classmates, she had swotted to the point of numbness. Now that the preliminary exams were over, she and Mairi celebrated by doing some window shopping. The chance for both girls to shop together came rarely, if at all. They lived in outlying villages and travelled each day into town, school, and then back to their homes. Today, it seemed they had all the time in the world.

It was a November lunchtime when shops and schools and offices would exchange populations with coffee shops and restaurants. The two girls huddled together down towards the streets' shop lights. They enjoyed the image they presented, the nonchalant scarves swung over their shoulders, the jaunty balancing tricks with books and bags.

"You know," Mairi piped up suddenly, "James does like you - a lot! I know that because he told me himself."

"He didn't!" Donna protested. And then, "Did he?"

"Right. The truth?"

"The truth." Donna pushed Mairi jokingly as they walked through the milling crowds outside the town's largest department store. Its rosy tinted windows glowed suggestively.

"Right. Watch - my - lips. I told him, 'Donna likes you.' He said, 'I know. I've been told that before.' "

"And?"

"And he said, 'I like her. Nice dark hair, nice brown eyes. Yeah, she's a bit of all right.' "

"Honestly?"

"Honestly! I reckon it won't be long before he asks you out. It'll restore your faith in the male species after that episode with Stewart Steele. That guy's bugged you so much - no one would blame you for reporting him to Pest Control!"

They both laughed and entered the shop. "I've to get tights for mum," Donna said, "I'm off upstairs. I'll be back in ten minutes - okay?"

"Fine," Mairi nodded, eyeing the cosmetic counter. "There's a perfume here I want to try out so that'll keep me occupied until you get back."

Both girls parted company and Donna, feeling quite lighthearted, skipped up the first few steps. Exams all over; James liked her; it could only get better. The only cloud on the horizon was Stewart Steele and she cringed at the thought of him. "Forget him," she said in a half whisper, turning around on the stairs to see if Mairi approved of the new perfume or not. It was good to have a friend like Mairi, she reflected.

Mairi was spraying the tester perfume on one wrist. She sniffed it, and as she laid down the tester perfume Donna saw, from her vantage point, that her hand had closed over a small bottle on the counter before her. Making as if to sneeze, she deftly slipped the small bottle into her pocket and, at the same time, pulled out her hanky to blow her nose, thus giving the whole scene a genuine unsuspicious cover.

Donna could feel her neck prickling as though with the electricity that hangs strongly, oppressively, in the air before a giant storm. "Oh, no!" she whispered.

She had actually witnessed her best friend, Mairi, shoplifting. She wanted to scream the fact into the noise and warmth and bustle of the shop, if only to convince herself it was really true. Instead, she woodenly propelled herself to the first floor and made her purchase.

She felt terribly alone. Mairi, shoplifting. The words squirrelled round in her mind, gathering and repeating themselves in a mocking dance. She remembered Mairi's curious fingering of those pearl-drop earrings of hers. She heard Katie's voice Look at you, Mairi, never lacking for anything."

Now she understood why Mairi always had the latest make-up, jewellery and perfume - all these little things you could, oh-so-easily, slip into a pocket. Donna clenched her teeth, tightened every muscle in her body in an attempt to still the shivering. Eventually, panic died down to a steady background of misery.

"Donna! I've been waiting for ages downstairs for you!" Mairi's bright voice, bright eyes, wide smile, assaulted Donna as she whirled round to face her.

"What?"

"Earth - Calling - Donna," Mairi intoned in a robotic voice. "Remember me? Mairi Martin? Have you developed amnesia all of a sudden?" Her voice was relaxed, teasing.

It was almost unbelievable for Donna to think that

Mairi could be so normal - how could she do it? The fragrance of the perfume still hung around Mairi, but for Donna, the day had definitely turned sour. Words stuck in her as she fumbled around weakly for something to say. What could she say?

"Oh! Um...yes...oh, I need to go to the baby section.... nearly forgot! Listen, I'll catch up, you go on ahead if you have things to do." Donna swiftly turned on her heel and soon disappeared behind a rail of pink dresses, much to the astonishment of a rather mystified Mairi.

For Donna, the rest of the day passed in a daze. Bumping into the S.S. gang, and being teased, didn't add up to a 'fun' type of day. By the time she got home, Donna was definitely bad company. At the tea table she remained distracted and sullen. Her mum, putting it down to teenage moodiness, was about to have none of it.

"Listen to me, Donna," she said as she dished up the fried fish, "I'm pregnant, forty, fat and fed-up. I'm really tired at the end of every day. I don't expect to come home to this type of behaviour. Now snap out of it and eat your tea. Do you want apple juice?"

"No thanks!" Donna's face was tingling with anger as she went on. "Look, Mum, am I usually moody? Have you ever thought I may need help? You can only talk baby, baby, baby! I'm sick of it! I'm not jealous, I'm looking forward to the baby. But, for Pete's sake, I *need* too."

"Oh, don't be so melodramatic." Her mother's voice was school-teacherish. "Right, what are your *needs*?"

"Oh, nothing. Forget it. Just forget I ever mentioned it."

"If it's that Stewart Steele," her mother persisted with an air of great patience, "just tell me and I'll..."

"Yes mum! Yes, it's him and it's a lot more besides." Donna looked up to meet her mother's frowned expression. "Life is just very mixed-up just now. That's all! I need time to think." Her voice trailed off, and they resumed their meal in silence.

It wasn't silence within though, for in Donna's mind, the wheels of thought were whirling around at alarming speed, throwing together bits of information and spitting out ugly, unthinkable conclusions. She felt the colour draining from her face.

The implications of the scene that was filtering through her mind hit her one by one; slowly, then in a rush. Stewart Steele, although he had blocked her way that day, it didn't prove that he had taken anything. Donna recalled clearly asking Mairi to hold her schoolbag whilst she ran ahead to give Katie her guitar. Mairi had been alone with the schoolbag.

"Come on, eat," Donna's mother said coaxingly. "Granny made oatcakes and barley bread this afternoon. She had health-food habits long before it became the 'in' thing!"

"Mmmm."

"Better than cotton-wool bread, isn't it?"

"Sorry? Oh, yes." Donna replied blankly, but in her mind there was a silent plea, "Mairi. Oh, no. No!"

Anger and loneliness gnawed inside. She felt the urgent need to talk to someone. But to whom? To Mairi? Never! Was there no-one? What about Stewart? He'd probably laugh, or yell...maybe even do both! No, she couldn't talk to him.

Suddenly and clearly, she thought of Rachel. Rachel, so sure that Stewart wasn't a thief. Rachel, so right.

6
BY THE FIRESIDE

Dishes done, excuses made, Donna set out briskly for Rachel's house. Walking helped to clear her muddled mind. There was no moon, but the stars were out, keen and sharp as the breeze that tugged at her jacket.

As she walked, the sky began to change. At first, there was only a pale light in the northern sky, then, so slowly, the pulsating, flickering band of light began to broaden and deepen and climb steadily in the sky. Soon other streamers in the very delicate pastel shades of violet and green and blue, but always predominantly white, grew brighter, higher, stronger. The Northern Lights. Searchlights. Incomparable.

'What a beautiful, beautiful world - and what a mess of people,' she thought sadly as she came to Rachel's lovely, well-built house. The outside doorlight welcomed her onwards and she noticed thankfully that Stewart's motor bike was nowhere to be seen.

Knocking twice, Donna went straight into the house. (On the island, only salespeople and tourists knocked and waited for someone to come to the door.) In she went and found Rachel dozing by the open fire in the sitting room.

The room was cosy and interesting all at the same time, and spoke far more eloquently of Rachel than she could herself. The walls displayed many pictures and paintings, most of which depicted true island life. There were fishermen, peatcutting, sheepfank, haymaking scenes. There was a beautiful picture showing a family reading the Bible together. There were some black and white shots, showing soberly dressed, solemn people who never smiled at the camera. These pictures retained a fascinating attraction for Donna as she went around each one in turn. By the hearth stood a pair of huge china cats, whilst all kinds of books lay scattered, some on shelves, some on the table, and a few favourites on the mantelpiece. On Rachel's lap lay her Bible, open, worn and - to Rachel - her most treasured possession of all.

Donna sat down gingerly but the creak from the old armchair woke the old woman and she looked alarmed - but only for a moment. "Oh, I'm sorry, Rachel. I didn't mean to waken you," Donna said quickly.

"Forty winks, don't tell anyone!" Rachel teased, struggling to sit upright. It was a lovely smile her old mouth gave. "Now, you take off your things, dear. It is cold outside. Come and warm yourself by the fire here."

Donna rubbed her hands together in the heat of that fire and soon warmed up.

"I am sorry if it's Stewart you are wanting. He is out just now at Duncan's loom-shed filling bobbins for him. He gets a little something for helping out and himself and Duncan get along very well." Rachel smiled and waited for Donna's answer.

"No, Rachel, I didn't come to talk to Stewart." Pausing, Donna swallowed hard. "I...I came to see you, Rachel...to talk to you about a few things."

Where could she begin though? She couldn't even put

a first sentence together. Words failed her.

Rachel seemed to sense her unease, and asked about Donna's father.

"He's fine, Rachel. He's hoping to be home at the end of January for three months, to be there when the baby comes along. I'm dying to see him again!"

"And tell me, how is your mother?"

Donna laughed at she thought of her. "Oh, she's just fine - huge though! I keep falling over every time she 'bumps' into me!"

Rachel laughed, but the laughter developed into an awful paroxysm of coughing. Donna got up and patted her on the back till she got her breath back.

"Don't you think you should see a doctor about that cough of yours, Rachel?" Donna asked, feeling very concerned for her.

"Och, I have been already," Rachel replied as she tried to get her breath back. "I have to go to the hospital for an X-ray, next week. I will go over to the town with Stewart, on the school bus."

Donna felt relieved that Rachel was being cared for. "That's good, Rachel. They'll soon have you as right as rain." She met Rachel's gaze and fell silent.

For a few moments they sat in companionable silence and listened to the homely sounds of the fire, as busy flames licked around the peats, creating a fantasy-land of images. Eventually Donna broached the dreaded subject.

" I don't really know how to say this Rachel. You see ...I...I was wrong about Stewart. He...he didn't take my calculator - or anything else for that matter. I'm really, really sorry I blamed him."

She glanced nervously at Rachel. The older woman's stillness contrasted with her own nervous prattle. "I don't blame you if you can't forgive me."

"Donna, Donna. If you only knew how much God has forgiven me - then you would understand how easy it is for me to forgive you now. In Christ, God offers forgiveness for all our sins, no matter how unforgivable they seem to other people. You see, dear, it is not those who deserve God's forgiveness who get it. The opposite. It was while we were sinners, complete strangers to God, that he loved us. So, of course I forgive you, Donna. You do not even need to tell me anything else - I understand."

But Donna had a great need to tell Rachel about everything that lay so heavy on her heart and mind. The old woman sat quietly and listened until the last word was said.

Donna concluded, "How can I ever trust Mairi again? Or anybody else? I really looked..." She felt her mouth all twisted as she continued. "I looked up to Mairi. She was everything I wanted in a friend. You just can't trust anybody!"

There was a short silence until Rachel began softly, "Donna, you've been very hurt, I know. And, yes, sometimes we do put our friends on a...what is the word...a pedestal. We look to our fellow human beings to fulfil a need in ourselves. Do you understand?"

"Yes, but that's okay for you Rachel. You have faith, you know. But for someone like me, well, it's hard to believe all that."

Rachel pushed back a stray curl of white hair. "Once, Donna, I was young just like you. Then, a crisis came, I called on Jesus and he was there, alive! Oh, I did not see him with my eyes, but Donna, I found that two thousand years had not aged him one bit! He still had the same power to change the lives of men and women. He could change your friend. He could change you."

There was a little silence, through which the old grandfather clock ticked solemnly.

"I don't want to be changed," Donna thought, "but Mairi could sure do with some inner transplant."

"With Christ at the centre, your whole world can begin to make sense." Rachel's tired eyes danced with sudden amusement. "Now, who taught me to be such a preacher!"

Donna didn't want her to stop talking. "Rachel, when you say 'crisis' - what do you mean?"

"It is so hard...so hard to put into words. It is not that my English will let me down, but there are some things that are difficult to put in any language!"

A look of mutual understanding passed between them as Rachel continued.

"Yes, I was young, happy - with a very handsome fiancee."

"You were engaged?"

"Yes. Norman was...well, I'll leave that just now. Anyway, I had my fill of these exciting things, but then...I don't know..."

She leaned forward and poked at the fire with a pair of tongs.

"Sometimes, I felt such a restlessness inside me. As if there was something in my life that was not complete. Even the happy times."

She cupped one hand as if holding something. "I felt as if these times were like a pile of dry sand that I was holding in my hand. No matter how hard I tried to hold on, the sand just trickled through my fingers, until there was none left.

"The War broke out. Norman was called up. I found work in a munitions factory on the mainland - we all felt we should do our bit. Things changed. We were all frightened then. Frightened for ourselves, frightened for our country, but most of all frightened for boyfriends, husbands, sons, fathers, brothers, cousins. Everybody had someone to be anxious about.

"I began to want a lasting peace. Something which did not depend on what was going on around me. Something which did not depend on other people. Something which would cast off all my fear."

Donna stared at her, spellbound. "And...?"

"And...and then I got news that Norman had become seriously ill in a prisoner-of-war camp in Italy. I did not even know that he had been captured! He had T.B. and with the conditions there, and so little good food...well..." Her voice became scarcely audible.

"Oh."

"I prayed so hard for him. I *willed* him to live. I tried to bargain with God."

Rachel stared at the fire in silent wonder.

"I said to God, 'If you will spare Norman, then I will follow you. All the days of my life.'

"Then, over the days and weeks that followed, there was a text from the Bible running through my mind. *What is that to thee? Follow thou me.*

"At first, it seemed so cruel. Norman was everything to me. But then...then I began to see that God was putting me to the test. Would I still follow him, even if the...the unthinkable happened?"

Donna nodded, but not with understanding.

"The funny thing was, Donna," Rachel turned to her. "I just could not resist the love of Christ. It drew me. In the end there was nothing I could do but say to God, 'Here I am. Do what you will. I want to be yours, whatever.' "

"And Norman?"

"News of his death came shortly after I asked God into my life. But he had actually died a week before that. Strange isn't it?"

"I'm sorry. That's awful."

"I often wonder," Rachel said softly, "if Norman remained an outsider from God's kingdom."

Donna wondered what that meant. Again the words of Katie's song re-echoed in her mind.

By this time, the fire was dying low. Rachel arranged the last few peats around the embers whilst Donna got up to refill the bucket. She returned to find Rachel standing by the sideboard.

"I have made this for the baby, dear. Take it now, although it is early yet. Take it tonight and remember me when you wrap the baby in it."

She put the crocheted white blanket into a bag and handing it to Donna, she added, "I have sat so many nights crocheting in bed when the arthritis and coughing is so bad that I cannot sleep. That blanket has passed many hours for me."

"Thanks. That's brilliant. I can't wait to see this blanket covering a heap of wee bitty baby!"

Rachel smiled, and then faced Donna squarely. "There is something that you have to do, Donna."

"Stewart?"

"Yes. It is him you have wronged. You know that. So,

although it will be hard for you..."

"I'll have to apologise, right?" Donna said. "Yes... yes, I will."

She left Rachel's house, knowing just how difficult that would be.

7

MELTING THE ICE

As Donna made her way out of the house, she noticed that the Northern Lights had disappeared. The cool November night had now tossed a cloak of iridescent frost over everything, and she wanted to get home quickly. Hurrying past the barn door, Donna felt a sudden, tight grip on her shoulder and she was shoved heavily against the barn wall and held there against her will.

A dozen pulses pounded within her. Her first thought was to scream out loud, but no sound came. In the partial light cast by Rachel's outdoor light, she could see Stewart Steele's face. His eyes were fixed, never leaving her face.

"Right, Donna Macdonald. I've had it with you!" His voice was a whiplash of ice-on-anger. "Just what do you think you're doing snooping around here? Trying to get more murky details about me to spread round the school? Well, you've got some nerve, blabbermouth, but this time you're not going to get away with it - no way, Donna!" And he gave her an extra shove against the cold stone wall just to prove his point.

"I came to talk to Rachel. That's all. *That's all*."

"That's all! That's enough! I've never hit a girl before, but I wouldn't mind making an exception to the rule. Right now! Only that would be playing into your hands. You'd run home to Mummy-land and she'd have me whipped into a detention centre before the week was out."

"Oh, don't be so stupid!" She wriggled out of his grasp. "Look, what harm could I possibly do by just talking to your aunt?"

"As if you didn't know! Last time you had a talk with her, you blabbered all over the school that I was illegitimate. Well, they won't be stuck now when it comes to calling me names, will they? Will they?"

"Look, you're making a mistake."

"Don't patronise me. I don't have to take it. Oh girl, if gossiping was an Olympic sport, you'd be odds-on for a medal, wouldn't you?"

She could feel uncontrolled tears oozing down her face. "I swear I didn't tell anyone, except..."

"Except who?"

"Oh, no," she thought, "oh no...she couldn't have..."

"Who?"

"Mairi Martin."

"Oh, I get it," he was quick to retort. "Now we move onto Phase Two; blame the best friend routine. Do you really think I'm going to fall for that? I'm not from another planet you know - you must think I'm dead stupid! Rachel *trusted* you. How could you? Why didn't you print it all in the local newspaper? It would have had the same effect."

Donna could feel goose-pimples break out all over her. "I didn't know that she would. I only told her because she asked. I told her not to tell anyone!" She buried her face in her hands, trying to sort out the jumbled confusion of pluses and minuses. What was the point of holding anything back? But what about Mairi?

She pulled up her collar to protect her face from the

bitter gusts of wind that stung any exposed skin like the smack of a cross hand. Condensation of expelled air that coated each fibre of woven wool in her jacket created a warm dampness against her lips. She couldn't find the right words.

The long, wordless, silence was eventually broken by Stewart. "Oh, you're a total waste of time. Why do I bother?" He wheeled round and took a few paces before staring sullenly at the moonlight peeping out from behind dark clouds.

Walking over to him, she felt her whole being tremble. Not facing him entirely, but standing near enough, she began to speak, very faintly at first but gradually strengthening.

"Stewart...I, well, I was wrong. About you, I mean. I... I was wrong, all along." Twice she tried to carry on, but her tongue felt warped and thick.

"Carry on, I'm enjoying this."

She glanced nervously at Stewart's face. The stillness of him, the firm set of his mouth, suddenly made it all the harder to speak. She tried again.

"I think - well, I've no proof - I think I know who stole the calculator. And maybe that person stole the other things. I don't know. I just don't know."

"Who is the latest poor beggar you're accusing?"

"I can't tell you. Please don't ask me!"

"I have a *right* to know, for Pete's sake! Time after time, when anything went missing, I was pronounced guilty by judge and jury - without even a trial. Wasn't I?"

She tasted the bitterness of the words hurled at her. "Yes."

"Okay, so you probably started the rumours. Or your mother. But some rat was stealing all the time, letting me take the rap for it. Who? Who was it?"

"Mairi Martin," she said, the two words almost choking in the dry thickness of her throat.

"Oh, c'mon! Do I look as if I came down with the last shower?"

"I might be wrong. That's why I didn't want to tell you. I was wrong about you, and look where it got me." The stupid tears were still falling and she wiped them furiously with the back of her hand.

"Wow! When it comes to ladling out blame, you're second to none, Donna."

"Please - listen! I saw Mairi today - stealing, when we went shopping together. I .... I couldn't say anything to her - it all seemed so unreal. She stole a bottle of perfume and just carried on as if nothing had happened."

Donna stopped momentarily and glanced nervously at Stewart to see his reaction. She wanted him to believe her. It was so important. He just had to know the truth - but would he believe her?

"I've spent most of today thinking about it, Stewart. I'm not trying to blame someone else. This is the truth. See, I remembered how Katie said that day how Mairi never lacked for anything. I remembered all the new earrings, perfumes, make-up, tapes, pens - lots of little things you could easily slip into a pocket."

She brought out a hanky, wishing she could keep her tears till later on, when she was alone.

"Stewart, I'm so sorry. I don't...didn't like you very much - if at all. It was too easy to blame you. I wanted it to be you. I figured you deserved it! But now - I see things differently. And...and I remember how I left my bag with Mairi that day when I ran to give Katie her guitar."

His eyes met hers. Each of them seemed to read the other's anxiety. The same genuine confusion.

"I'd forgotten something too, till just now." Stewart moistened his lips, seeming uncertain as whether to carry on.

"What?"

"See, when I came here first, I went along to the disco. Well anyway, that Mairi creature came onto me pretty heavy, all over me like a rash, wanting a date and all that stuff."

He seemed oddly embarrassed to have spoken in such a way, and so avoided Donna's searching look.

"See, I wasn't interested. I told her to dig a hole and bury herself. Or words to that effect."

"Nice!"

"Definitely not nice. Definitely not my scene, that kind of girl."

"I won't ask you what is 'your scene'!"

"And I won't tell you."

She could not decide if he was joking or not. There was a spark in his eye, which seemed to say he was teasing her. She imagined how he could have been if they had got to know one another in a friendly way, and the knowledge was painful. She pulled herself together.

"I'll never, never forgive her! When I ranted and raved about you...you know, stealing...she never once said anything to stop me. Never. She could have said, 'Hang on, it might not be him.' But no, she egged me on. 'Who else could it be?' she'd say. 'Nothing ever went missing till he came along.' Oh, what a *fool* I've been."

Stewart did not reply. She stole a sideways look at him. His profile showed his eyes crinkled at the corners and unusually glistening.

"Okay, share the joke, Stewart."

"Well, well," he said turning round to face her. "Here you are Donna, not willing to forgive Mairi, but you still expect me to forgive you, isn't that right? Typically selfish!"

Donna was grateful that the dim light would not reveal her reddening face. "Yes. You're right. It's something we could both work on, I suppose. I'll try to forgive Mairi and...well, you could try to forgive me. I know I have a few faults..."

"A few? Do you want me to draw up a register of all of them? That won't be hard, Donna!"

"Oh, shut up. You're bad for my ego."

"It's fairly taken a battering, hasn't it? Your ego, I mean."

"Since you arrived on the scene, Stewart - yes. I know you'll hold this up in evidence against me, but honestly, till you came along, I don't think anyone ever *hated* me before. At least not openly."

"Wasn't hard. The K.G.B. reporting back to the Kremlin. The Ministry of Propaganda and all that. It's not difficult to hate *that*."

They both looked at each other, communicating without words. After a while Donna said quietly, "What about this forgiveness thing? Can we both work on it?"

"You speak for yourself. Count me out. I'll forgive you only when I'm good and ready."

"Until then, grovel. Is that it?"

"Got it first time, Donna! Eat humble pie. It'll do you good."

Despite herself, a hint of amusement crossed Donna's face. "If you think I'm going down on my knees and beg, forget it. Anyway, I enjoyed the fight - it's boring trying to be nice to you! Tell me when to put away the boxing gloves, will you?"

But one look at his face made her realise that it would take a lot more than a few light-hearted quips to repair the damage she had caused between them. Perhaps Stewart would never even want her friendship now.

"Goodnight, Stewart," she said quietly as she turned to go. She paused, hoping for an answer but none came out of the darkness. Looking back, she met his grave, almost brooding gaze.

"Yeah - goodnight - although I'm not sure you deserve anything good."

With that he left, the sound of his boots mingling with the whine of the wind. She turned and headed for home, his last words to her still ringing in her ears.

8

REVENGE

Monday morning at school found Donna battling with her emotions, as the weekend had not blurred the edges of her betrayed feelings.

Mairi, unaware of Donna's hostility, was in an exceptionally chatty mood. "Hey, Donna! Pick me as your partner for the Geography project - okay?" she said light-heartedly, as they ambled towards the classroom.

"Um...yeah, Mairi...okay," Donna replied while inspecting the contents of her schoolbag closely to avoid eye contact. "Partner," she thought silently, "you must be joking!"

Sitting down at their tables, Donna faced a further shock as Mairi began, "You'll never, *ever*, believe this, girls. Stewart Steele asked me to go to the disco with him tonight! Wow - I feel as if all my Christmases have come at once!"

She paused for a reaction and, as the other girls supplied in plenty, Donna said nothing. The realisation of this new turn of events swept across her like a forest fire. She felt doubly betrayed. How could it be? Surely Stewart must hate Mairi as much as she did? How could he do this to her?

Mairi, unaware of Donna's reaction, began to relate a few more details to her captive audience. "Yes. It's true!

He came down to the Youth Club - late on Friday night, and he wouldn't take 'no' for an answer. I just can't wait!"

Her eager chatter - which often earned her the title of 'Motor Mouth' - was silenced as the teacher arrived and quickly got them all paired and settled into their project work.

After class, Mairi teamed up with Donna again, as usual. "Hey! What's with you this morning? You've hardly spoken a word and why on earth did you choose Katie - of all people - for the project?"

Mairi's questions opened the door wide to a torrent of angry answers, but Donna could only stammer "Um...well."

"She spoke. Welcome back to the human race!" Mairi said, and Donna hated her bright eyes, her laughter, the way she tossed her hair back. She hated her, full stop.

"Does it bother you that I'm going out with Stewart?" Mairi asked, giving Donna a deep and meaningful look.

Donna was too quick in her reply.

"Mairi, you know I can't stand the guy! Maybe he'll finally get off my back if he's taken up with you," she said, quickening her pace.

"Don't worry, Donna," Mairi said reassuringly, "I'll see that he leaves you alone from now on."

Mairi was so smug, as if already assuming a certain ownership of their mutual acquaintance. Donna could only smile weakly and offer a curt 'see you' over her shoulder, before going into her Gaelic class.

November freshness pressed through the partly open-ed classroom windows and seemed to dispel the heavy humid weight of her emotions. Outside the trees were winter-leaved with blackbirds. Donna listened to the birds making excited twittering noises, and watched them as they fell off the branches into space. Their perfect, curved wings would then lift them on the air.

'Lucky them,' she thought enviously. 'They can take off and fly away when they like. No conflicts, no disturbing thoughts, no betraying friends.'

Late afternoon found her making her way alone to the school bus. Moments later she sat wrapped in her thoughts as the bus took her to the comfort of her home.

Darkness was already beginning to fall all around. The bright glow of the town gave way to the hazy orange glow of the sodium street lights which marked out the villages that lay between the town and her home. In the distance, landing lights went on at the small airport to guide in the plane which passed overhead.

All around, as far as the eye could see, lay the drab, damp November moorland - mostly flat and uninteresting, but here and there the distant hills cut their silhouette into the early evening sky. Passing yet another village, she could just make out the form of scattered houses and crooked stone walls swathed in the peat-smoke haze which curled unceasingly from the chimneys. Donna stared down at the book which lay opened, but unread, in her lap.

"Can I see, Donna?" Stewart Steele slid into the seat beside her. He lifted the curtain of her hair aside and looked at her book. "Mills and Boons? Will it give me any hints on romantic talk?"

She could only stare. How could he sit beside her? How could he pretend there was nothing wrong? She tackled the anger that rose sharply within her, and aimed for a light-hearted tone.

"You mean for your date tonight?" she asked.

"You heard?"

"Mmmm. I run a detective agency as a sideline!"

"Be serious. I want a man-to-man talk."

"That'll be a bit difficult, biologically speaking," she quipped, and he laughed and leaned back in the seat. Then his expression became unreadable.

"I went down to the Youth Club after our little chat. I started chatting Mairi up. Turned the charm full on."

"Oh, you've got a supply then?"

"Hey, good one, Donna!"

"You know, I think I could cope with your nastier side better than the fully-turned-on charm side."

"So, what's new?"

"We've seen the worst of each other, haven't we, Stewart?" Donna said and Stewart nodded in agreement.

They watched each other in the dusky darkness. The minutes ticked by and then, somewhere in that long, slow quiet, the gulf between them began to diminish. The silence between them grew so loud that eventually Donna looked away.

"Well... what do you think?" Stewart asked.

"I suppose I can't figure out why you're taking her out, of all people. I mean...I thought you didn't like her now that you know what I told you about her. Now you're asking her out! It just doesn't make sense."

Her voice serious now, she turned her head to face him and she waited, hoping for some response that would help her to understand.

"Don't you see *why* I'm doing it, Donna? How can you be so slow on the uptake? See, I figure I'll trap her into some kind of confession... I'll just string her along until I get the truth out of her. She's the pits, and that's all she deserves!" Stewart laughed mockingly, already anticipating the sweet taste of revenge.

But Donna - how could she respond? Part of her wanted to laugh out loud along with Stewart. Part of her felt strangely relieved that his reasons for the date were for revenge rather than romance. A part of her remembered Rachel. Would this be her way of dealing with Mairi?

The bus lurched and stopped, unloading a group of noisy school pupils and also several bobbins of yarn for the local weaving sheds. Donna watched as the shadows disappeared and blended into the darkness.

"Stewart, I don't think it would be your aunt Rachel's way, somehow. See, when I blamed you, she didn't try to get even or anything like that. She handled that situation in just the right way and I learned a lot that night."

"Sure, forgiveness and love and all that stuff," he answered quickly. "That would never work with a trash like Mairi. She deserves all she can get."

"Then I deserve...whatever it is you've got in mind."

"You're not on *her* side, surely?"

"No, but I've been trying to step back from the situation a bit today." Donna's laugh was shaky. "I spent the weekend hating Mairi, and then feeling guilty, and trying to forget, and then hating her all over again. And I thought of Rachel and thought of her faith."

"Oh no, you're not joining the God Squad, are you?"

He shook his head in mock disbelief, but it couldn't dispel the warmth of feeling between them. It was as if they had survived physical dangers together, and in their relief could share confidences, that they kept hidden from others.

"You're spending too much time with Katie, aren't you?" he went on, jokingly. "Good folk like her give us teenagers a bad name."

"Get real, will you?" she retorted. "I've no intention of becoming good-living, or whatever, but - I don't know how to explain this, but I feel I'm an open book as far as this...this Jesus is concerned. You know how you thought - probably still think - that I was a spoilt brat. I feel that he knows even more about me than that. He knows the hidden bits of selfishness. He knows all the grotty bits and still..."

"Go on."

"Katie said today that even when he knows the things you hide from anyone else, he would still accept you as his own. She said something like God's love knowing the very worst - and still loving. It reminded me of your aunt Rachel. She spoke about things like that too. It just made me think, that's all."

Stewart was not at all impressed and shrugged his shoulders.

Both got off the bus together and Stewart carried Duncan's bobbins to the weaver's shed, where the familiar 'clickety-clack' of the loom, and the bundles of finished tweed told the tale of a hard-working man. There they prepared to part, but strangely, neither knew what to say.

Finally, Donna said, "Sorry for the religious guidance lesson."

"That's okay. Welcome back to this century! That religious stuff was a Big Sell a hundred years ago when people were poor and uneducated."

"That's exactly what my mother says."

"Don't tell me your mother and I *agree* on something!"

"That's a turn-up for the books, isn't it?" Donna said and they both laughed. Stewart walked away, but turned round and called to her. "Tonight, I'm not bothered who's going to read my thoughts. I'm out for revenge, baby."

9

TRUTH ABOUT RACHEL

A distinct sadness had gripped Donna - a sadness that would not shake off, but grew as the hours went by. Having parted with Stewart the previous evening, Donna - now back at school the following morning - was eager to discover the outcome of the 'date'. What had happened? Had Mairi owned up? There was no way of knowing, as both Stewart and Mairi were absent from school.

It was a stormy day, the first day of December. Wild noise and turbulence rose outside the classroom windows. The light darkened, the wind howled and whined, the rain whirled in and whipped the faces of the local housewives struggling downtown to reach the shops.

As Donna looked out of the window, she was full of thoughtfulness. Again the feeling of persistent, unspecific doubt returned. She searched her mind. What was it? Why did she feel so restless, so uncomfortable? Was it a concern that Stewart and Mairi had got on a shade too well? Or was it the ache of regret for a disappearing friendship and a misplaced trust.

At the lunchtime break, however, she saw Stewart appear and make for a corridor at the back of the school. She made excuses to her friends and followed him into the deserted corridor. As she came towards him, she saw that he was leaning against a window, his head bent forward.

He looked grim and unutterably weary.

"Stewart? Hi," she said, attempting a smile. But he looked away, and the smile faded abruptly from Donna's eyes. "Stewart, what is it? What's wrong?"

He swallowed hard and stared out the window. "It's ...Rachel. I've...I've been to the hospital to see her."

Suddenly, the impatience and earlier uneasiness gathered in a jet of apprehension. All at once, it became urgent and immediate for Stewart to turn and explain things to her. She tried again.

"But, but...I thought Rachel was just in yesterday for tests? She's...they've not kept her in, have they?"

He nodded. "She's got...uh, you know..."

His eyes were dark with shadows, the mouth too firmly controlled. Outside, huge drops of rain were hitting the windows with hard, vicious impact and Donna wondered how all the big things in life can slip themselves into such small conversations.

Something like pain frayed the edges of his voice. "They don't know yet where it started but it's spread to her hip bones and her lungs. It's too far advanced to try operations or drugs or anything like that. It's too late really - for anything."

Donna did not speak for a moment. She stood close to him with her head turned towards the window while her shock-stupefied mind struggled to sort out meanings.

"Stupid woman! Stupid, stupid woman!" There was a trace of ugliness in the set of his mouth as he kicked a radiator viciously. "If only she had listened to me! I told her to go to the doctor dozens of times. Why didn't I *make* her go at the beginning? I shouldn't have listened to her!"

"Oh, Stewart, please...please, don't," Donna pleaded.

Her heart seemed to give a little jerk of pity and tenderness.

"Darn her!"

She searched his face. He looked so different when he was vulnerable like that. Boldly, and very gently, she put her hands on either side of his face as if he were a little child to be comforted. She wished there was such a thing as healing hands and that her hands could heal the hurt inside him.

"Stewart, I'm sorry, I'm so sorry. But please, don't blame yourself. And maybe, who knows? - even if she had gone to the doctor earlier - maybe it would still have been too late. Only God knows."

"Don't *mention* God. Leave him out of it, right?" His voice was harsh and Donna dropped her hands. "Tell me, where is God now? For Pete's sake, Rachel is only in her late sixties. She's got pain, it's hard for her to breathe properly, and she doesn't have much time left. Where's her God hiding in all this?"

"I don't know. I just don't know." That wasn't anything to say, but there was nothing else she could say. "I wish I knew," she added quietly.

His voice softened a little. "She...she looked so ill and small and frail, lying in that hospital bed today. I...I couldn't even stay with her, I thought I'd crack up, so I told her I had to get back to school. She knew I was lying...she knew."

The words dropped between them into a small silence. There were tears in his eyes, brimming, but not falling. He looked at her for the first time and for a little time they were trapped in each other's gaze.

"The thought of going back to that room and trying to

make conversation with her - I can't do it!" His voice, now a husky whisper, began to crack.

"You'll have to, Stewart." Donna felt once more, deep inside her, the warm twist of pity. "I mean, I'm trying to understand what you're going through. And it's hard. But it'll be even harder to look back with regret. It's a time when you should be closer than ever before. Stewart, don't build walls between you and Rachel."

Stewart was silent, and Donna continued gently, "I know that, for Rachel, the sun rises and sets on you. Don't shut her out, because you can't cope with your own feelings."

The school bell rang, jarring into their multitude of thoughts, but Donna went on, "Have they told Rachel?"

Stewart blew his nose and replied, "Tomorrow. They'll tell her tomorrow, they say. Poor Rachel! How can you tell someone that they're dying of cancer? How can I face her Donna, when she knows and she knows that I know? I won't even be able to look at her."

They started walking unenthusiastically towards the classroom areas but, in her mind, Donna drifted back to her last meeting with Rachel. She thought of Rachel's words to her that evening. Out of these memories came a phrase which suddenly took on new meaning. "Take the shawl tonight, dear, and 'remember me' whenever you wrap the baby in it!" Something new dawned from the recalling of these words. Perhaps the doctors wouldn't have to tell Rachel anything. Surely Rachel had known - long ago. She turned to share the thought with Stewart, but he had already begun talking. "I suppose I should tell you...you'll want to know about the date, I suppose."

"I did. But I don't now," she replied. "Since last

Friday I have been taken up with so many problems. Just so caught up in life's fever. Hate, misery, anger, self-pity. You name it, and if it's a negative emotion, I've gone through it! The whole gamut of emotions from A to Z. And now it all seems so stupid."

"When you think of dying, and a death, is that what you mean?"

"Mmmm. We work, we eat, we sleep; work, eat, sleep; we worry, we laugh, we envy, we scheme, we plan. And for what? It's all going to come to nothing in the end."

"Don't go all profound on me, girl. Stick to the scheming and planning bit. I can cope with that."

They were already late for their separate classes and Stewart said hurriedly, "I sent Mairi on one big ego trip, laid on the flattery with a trowel. See, I wasn't worried about Rachel then, because I thought she'd be out of hospital after the morning tests. Anyway, to cut a long story short, I ended the evening by telling Mairi that I really admired her style of shoplifting."

He smiled wanly as he continued, "I told her that a spoilt brat like you deserved to have a Judas as best friend. Then I told her a few home truths and sent her packing. Her date ended on a very sour note."

"Oh, that's awful. I should be pleased, I know, but..."

His face twisted into a little smile, but there was no sound of victory in his words. "Mission accomplished. But don't bother with the medals."

He looked at her in silence. It was no longer the silence of shared emotions, but a pause charged with some new and disturbing elements that Donna did not quite understand. He looked so different. Different in expression, different, somehow, in appearance. And then, as he turned to go, she realised something. The gold cross earring was gone.

And she remembered that look he had given her, nursing it through the rest of the day. Forgetting the angry tirade that met her when she eventually made her way to class, she tried to freeze that frame of him in her mind, wanting to file it like a precious snapshot.

10

A COMFORTING WORD

Another long school day had dragged past. Stewart's news was the only thing that mattered to Donna now. She stood waiting for the school bus.

In the western sky, the December sun touched the rim of the earth. The sun was heavy, pulsating with light, touching the school buildings with pink. All around the sky's edge ran a faint pink glow, above that was yellow, and then there was purple shadows lingering in the more colourless expanse further from the sun.

She was admiring the scene when, in the distance, she saw a lone figure approaching and recognised Stewart long before he reached her.

"Hello, Stewart," she said quietly, "how's Rachel today?"

Stewart shuffled around awkwardly and kicked about a few loose stones. "Well, I...I haven't actually been to see her - yet." He took a deep breath, like a swimmer before a dive. "A favour, Donna?"

"Depends if it's legal."

"Very funny! I, well, I was wondering if you would come with me to the hospital?" Urgency had made him lower his voice. "Please. I need *someone* to come with me. I can't cope by myself."

Donna tried to put a smile in her voice. "Changed

days, Stewart. You need *me?*"

"Rachel knows you. She likes you," he said with the same soft stubbornness. "Don't go searching for compliments, girl. Are you coming or not?"

The school bus was filling up and would soon be gone. "I'll go," she said, realising just how difficult that would be. "Yes, of course I'll go."

With relief, Stewart managed the smallest of smiles. "Thanks - I knew you would."

Walking through the freshly fallen autumn leaves, their minds were distracted by the sounds underfoot, and their eyes watched the dancing leaves. The sting of the wind brushed their exposed skin like the cold touch of steel and Donna pulled the collar of her jacket up around her neck. She shivered. Was it the cold that made her shiver, or was it her visit to Rachel?

On reaching the long, lonely corridors of the hospital, Donna stopped briefly, phoned her mother to explain the situation, then rejoined Stewart who led her to the Medical Wing. Stopping outside Room 12, they gave each other an uneasy glance. Donna's heart began to thump loudly, and she felt the colour drain from her face. Stewart stiffened, composed himself and went in, leaving Donna to follow like a shadow behind him.

"Oh, Stewart *and* Donna, isn't that good! You're both here."

Rachel was in bed, propped up on pillows. Donna noticed that her skin had the stretched pallor of exhaustion, but the eyes, despite the smudge of sleepless nights beneath them, were alive and radiant.

"Come in, come in! Look, sit down beside me here. I am so glad that you have come - and both of you together!"

Neither Donna nor Stewart seemed able to speak or even find the smallest voice to speak with. "How...how are you?" Donna finally asked in a voice which seemed to come, disembodied, from somewhere else.

"Och, I am not too bad. I am not worse than I was at home, just tired - very, very tired, and out of breath with all this coughing. The nurses here - they are kind and they are taking good care of me."

Her conversation stopped suddenly, as a severe bout of coughing left her gasping for breath and in apparent pain. Donna called the nurses who quickly came to attend to Rachel.

Stewart stood at the window with his back to them all, looking out on the darkening sky, where a lone star shone, remote and cold and indifferent.

Rachel sank back on to the pillow, and rested for a few moments. Stewart turned towards her, looking uncomfortable and despairing. Donna wished he would say something - anything - yet she could see just how difficult it was for him to cope. It was, once again, Rachel who spoke, now in quiet, hushed tones, pausing frequently for breath.

"Stewart, don't you know that I know how hard this must be for you!" and she lifted up a hand as if to silence the protest on his lips. "Just like yesterday. I knew it was hard for you."

She paused and Donna helped her to sip a little cold water. "Before the doctor came to tell me, I was reading the Bible. It was the story of old Simeon, when he held the little child Jesus. Simeon said, 'Lord, now let your servant depart in peace; according to your word; for my eyes have seen your salvation.' You see, this wonderful

Saviour, even when he was in the form of a little babe in
the arms of Simeon, took the dread of death away from
the old man's heart. He could then welcome death,
because his eyes had seen God's salvation. And that is
how I am."

Rachel looked at them in her serenity, then she turned
her attention to Donna.

"Even in the past few weeks the Lord has taught me so
much. Body hurt is nothing compared with mind hurt. And
I was really hurt by your mother's actions, Donna. I saw her
as out to destroy any chance Stewart had of settling
down."

Donna nodded, wordlessly.

"It was the dark night of my soul, I can tell you. It was
as if God had withdrawn himself. The hurt was not so
much in my bones. The hurt was where the heart was.
Then, one day, I felt as if the Lord was saying to me , 'I love
that person, too. I died for her as well as for you.'

"Then it was the easiest thing in the world to forgive.
And I prayed that you and Stewart would lose the bitterness there was between you and replace it with a warm
friendship. And he has, I can see that!"

Rachel looked out the window, at the sky now welling
up with night.

"You see how kind Jesus is? Nothing is too big for his
power. Nothing is too hard for his love."

"Then why is he letting you go through all this, huh?"
Stewart burst out angrily.

"Oh Stewart, I do not know *why,*" she answered. All
I know is that he has promised to be with me. Even today,
he showed me something."

Donna wanted to run away. She couldn't cope with

this. She tried to think of tomorrow - this afternoon would end. This day would end. She caught on to Rachel's words.

"The nurse wrote my temperature on her hand because she had not made up a chart for me. She said she would remember to write it down, because it was there, right in front of her all the time. And it reminded me," Rachel went on, "of a verse - *I have engraved thee on the palms of my hands*. God has me there, right in front of him. And not only written, but engraved. Deeply cut into his hands. It was through the pain of the Cross that my name was engraved there.

"So you see," she finished gently, "he will be with me in this valley of shadows."

'Valley of Shadows. Shadowland. Death's Dark Vale. Oh, Rachel...' Donna swallowed and stared hard at the tiled floor.

"I did have a little weep," Rachel admitted after a while. "I did think of the way life would go on without me. My pew at church will be filled by another. I'll not see your mother's new baby, Donna. I'll not see you both as adults."

She did not want pity. She was merely stating a fact. And, for the first time in her own life, Donna had a glimpse of the stabbing loneliness there could be for someone facing an imminent death.

Then Rachel turned to Donna and said softly, "But for me to live is Christ, to die is gain."

She had spoken words so nearly connected to her thinking, that Donna did not know how to react.

"Will the two of you promise me something?" Rachel asked after a long silence. "Can you come and have worship with me every day? I find it so hard to read, my eyes, you know."

They didn't 'know', but it was almost a relief to do something as straightforward as reading the Bible. Stewart fumbled through the pages with unfamiliarity, cleared his throat and read the twenty-third psalm. After the reading, Rachel lifted her hands a fraction, closed her eyes and prayed.

All the prayers Donna had ever heard had been well thought out, words carefully chosen, usually unemotional. Rachel's prayer was different. Words poured from her lavishly, inarticulately, a geyser of heartfelt thanks, unashamedly expressed. Like a bird on wing, her emotions were wheeling, darting, circling, wanting to keep flying for ever.

Afterwards, Donna opened her eyes, but Rachel's were still shut, as if the silent moment was very precious.

11
ARROGANCE OR IGNORANCE

In the two weeks that followed, Stewart and Donna experienced a curious happiness with Rachel. To be with Rachel for that daily visit was to have everything. It was to be in the right place at the right time. It was to see a physical life ebbing, and a spiritual life unfolding, full of bright promise. A golden December with chill nights and bright crisp days, and the sound of geese honking sadly, flying south.

"Senair - it's strange how I feel when I visit Rachel. I always feel sick to my stomach when I walk into that hospital. But, you know it's her who comforts us, and not the other way round!"

Donna, perched on the wee barn stool, watched her grandfather as he milked 'Sine', the brown and white cow. Senair milked her with a steady rhythm and paused from time to time, to transfer the warm, foaming milk from the small pail to the bucket behind him. 'Sine', content with Seanair's easy handling of her, licked up the grain and crunched the turnips, her big, brown eyes gazing solemnly around.

On cue, 'Piseag', the ginger barn cat came through and curved her body against Senair's leg, purring loudly. Senair smiled as he filled her saucer with milk, and set it down beside her.

As Donna gazed around her, the barn brought peace and ease to her mind. She loved its comforting smell - the dusty-sweet smell of the hay, the hot brown smell of the cow, the woolly smell of the sheep. The warm, sweet stillness was inviolated only by a jumping, wriggling, panting sheepdog, 'Dileas', who covered Donna in warm, wet licks of gladness.

"You know, Seanair, the folk from her church are so good to Rachel. Flowers, cards and they visit her in turn, as often as they're allowed to. Sometimes, though, she's too weak and they only let Stewart and myself see her."

Seanair eyed Donna curiously, a small mischievous smile running around the corners of his mouth. "Aye - maybe they think you're his girlfriend, Donna," he suggested with a twinkle in his eye.

"What - no way! Me and Stewart? No way, Seanair!" she responded swiftly, although she was quick to hide her reddening face by cupping her chin in her hands.

"Methinks the lady doth protest too much." Senair still remembered scatterings of Shakespeare.

"We're more like brother and sister. Sometimes we hardly speak to each other when Rachel is very tired. Other times, when we leave the hospital, we crack jokes - really stupid ones. Crazy, isn't it?"

"I suppose it's just a way of relieving tension," Senair said thoughtfully. He stripped the last drops of milk from the teats, stood up and straightened his cap.

"I don't think I could do what you're doing, Donna," he added, before lighting up his pipe. "I mean daily visiting of the dying, and all that."

"Oh, Seanair, that sounds *awful*. What if everyone felt that way? Rachel wouldn't see anyone."

"I suppose it's because I'd be reminded of my own mortality, or something like that. If she can get cancer, so can I. If she must suffer and die before her time, so may I."

"Well, her friends don't feel that way. They run a risk too. They're prepared to share the sadness. And the reminders of their own mortality, as you put it. Only they don't believe they're...uh...mortal - is that the word? They don't believe that death is the end."

"Well, I do," Senair said challengingly. "Everything that lives must die. Even a star must die."

"I think Rachel's 'star' will re-appear," Donna said with intensity. "I can't believe that it will go out forever."

"You're about as much fun as a funeral, my girl. Where's the laughter gone?"

Donna laughed and scratched the area around the little horns of the calf. He responded by forcing his blunt, velvety nose between the wooden bars of the stall, and licked her hand with his rough tongue. Her grandfather smiled approvingly at them, then to change the subject, asked, "Where's that Stewart boy staying now that Rachel is in hospital?"

"Oh, he's at John Campbell's, you know, the church elder. Stewart enjoys being there. He's pretty used to the 'no TV. on Sunday' routine, and all that stuff!"

The night was cold as they closed the heavy barn door behind them. Far above them hung the large, glittering stars. The moon looked shrunken with cold, and the churned up soil was frozen hard beneath their feet as they walked across to the old croft house.

"My, but it's cold out there tonight," Seanair said as he put the milk bucket down on the draining board, and ran the tap. "Donna's been great company though, telling me all about her friend, Stewart!"

Donna nudged him playfully as she dried her hands on the soft blue towel. Donna's mother didn't like the mention of Stewart's name and remained silent. Granny, halfway through sieving the milk, managed a faint smile, and asked, "How's he enjoying being at John's then? He'll surely feel a bit out of place with these religious folks, and their 'never on a Sunday' rules. Rather him than me!"

Donna's mother cleared her throat in embarrassment, because she spent Sunday catching up on the week's video-taped programmes. For her, the Lord's Day was merely an affliction to be endured. "It'll do the boy the world of good to live under a strict regime like that. Just what he needs to sort him out!"

"Actually, mum, he likes living there. I'm not saying he agrees with their faith and all that, but he sees it working in their lives. He sees their 'faith in action', I suppose," Donna added thoughtfully.

"In action!" her mother responded angrily, and wriggled in her chair to find a more comfortable position. "Do these people think they're 'oh-so-much better' than the rest of us...is that it? I don't know if it's arrogance or ignorance that makes these religious folk assume that they're somehow better than the rest of us! Okay, so we don't go to church, and we're not fanatic about family worship, and keeping the Lord's Day, and so on. But we try and do good. We don't harm anyone. I'm sure that's all God requires of us."

Granny agreed wholeheartedly, as she quickly went to rescue hot scones from the oven. "Some people need a crutch to lean on, that's all," was her contribution.

Senair, pipe in mouth, looked from wife to daughter to grand-daughter in turn. He always enjoyed these high flying discussions of theirs.

Donna was sufficiently fired up to respond to their challenge. "See Katie, for instance. She found a personal faith when she was only fourteen. How can that be a substitute, or a crutch?"

"What happened to her, then?" Senair was interested enough to remove the pipe from his mouth. He loved to know what people experienced and listened as a child being told an enchanting tale. His personal interest went no further.

"Well, Seanair," Donna began, "she'd wanted to become a Christian but didn't know what to do about it. Anyway, one day, her baby brother climbed too high and couldn't get down. He called for Katie and she stood beneath him and held out her arms so that he could jump safely into them."

She paused momentarily, feeling almost embarrassed as she saw Seanair's bored expression. He stuck his pipe back into his mouth and picked up his paper, but Donna was determined to finish off her story.

"It...it sort of occurred to her that God was just like that. Waiting, with outstretched arms for Katie to commit her life into his hands. So, she did."

"Not very exciting, that," Seanair said. "Not like, you know, the alcoholic woken at midnight from a drunken stupor with a text ringing in his ears. Or an atheist suddenly having a vision of being shaken over hell. That sort of thing."

"Oh, Seanair," Donna could not help laughing. "That

would mean that you had to wait for some great crisis, or dreadful vision, before you became a committed Christian. Katie says..."

"Here we go again," her mother muttered.

"Katie says that even when everything in our garden is rosy - even then, we should still become Christians. Because Jesus is Lord; because he exists; because it's all true. That's what she says, anyway," Donna concluded in a voice which still held a faint trace of embarrassment.

Granny brewed up some tea, and Donna's mother sighed. "Okay, Donna. Switch off all this religious talk. You're making my back worse."

Soon there were hot scones, cups of tea, oatcakes, crowdie and cream. Conversation meandered around this and that, but not really about anything that mattered so much to Donna as Rachel and the conversations by her bedside.

As Donna sat in the kitchen, listening to all the empty chatter, in her heart she longed to be beside Rachel, where everything made so much sense.

12
AN ANGRY CONFRONTATION

Leaving Seanair and granny's early enough for mum to get her usual and much needed early night, they found Mairi Martin waiting on their front porch. "Mairi," said Mrs Macdonald cheerfully, "what a nice surprise! Haven't seen you for a while. Come in for a cup of tea."

Mairi came in smiling, and eyed Donna, who busied herself by turning on the lamps in the lounge. "Haven't seen you for a while, Donna. Been a bit hectic lately."

Mairi sat down nervously on the edge of the sofa. Donna turned to face her and squirmed inwardly at the light, pretty voice and the dimpled smile. Mrs Macdonald brought their tea through, then went up to bed, excusing herself and leaving the girls to talk.

Mairi rattled on, eager to impress Donna with some sharp news. "Donna, have I got news for you! This will knock you for six." Donna heard that honey tone in her voice as she went on, "James wants to take you to the Christmas Eve dance at the Town Hall. Can you believe it? I mean, Donna, he usually goes out with older girls, but you seem to be his number one just now!"

Donna was annoyed at herself as she smiled at Mairi's flattering words. How could she fall for it, and yet how could she spit out what was really on her mind? She reminded herself of the conversation at Seanair's house earlier and about the qualities of inner goodness which mum had said were all that was required of us.

Stifling her rising anger at Mairi's confidence in their renewed friendship, she said flatly, "Well, yeah I'm pleased. He's an okay guy and I'll probably go."

"What'll you wear? You can borrow stuff from me if you like," Mairi said, flashing her ready smile. She was trying hard to win back Donna's favour.

Donna sipped the hot tea, and stared blankly at the few dying flames left from a once blazing fire. "I'll wear my new black dress I think but, no thanks, I won't borrow any of your things." She swallowed hard and added, "I don't go in for stolen stuff."

Only a few words said in a voice that was still calm, still reasonable, but without life. Without shifting her gaze, Donna could feel instantly the impact of what she'd said.

"What *are* you talking about, Donna?" Mairi finally asked after a long silence, but Donna moistened her lips and said nothing. Mairi flared suddenly, shrilly, into anger. "Stewart Steele's been talking to you. Hasn't he?"

Donna did not look up. She said in a flattened, neutral tone, "He may have done. But he didn't have to. I knew all along."

Again, silence. Donna looked up and saw that, for Mairi, comprehension was instant. "You know about the calculator?" Mairi asked.

"Yes. And about everything else," Donna said in a voice sharp with scorn.

All at once her composure shattered and the mound of inner goodness evaporated. Out spilled an angry tirade which grew in size and volume as she spoke.

"Mairi! How could you? How *could* you do this to me?

You're the lowest of the low, you know that? I thought you were my friend. Not only did you pinch all that stuff from the shops but - to steal my calculator! With a friend like you, who needs enemies?!"

"Look, I can explain," Mairi said despairingly.

"Oh, cut the hang-dog look. It doesn't wash with me!"

Donna knew she had lost her temper. The ice-cold shell of control that she had maintained over the last few weeks was now shattered. She knew it, and didn't care.

"You've really let me down, Mairi; *and*...if you ever think I'll be your friend again, well you can just think again! You even let me blame Stewart and that was pretty cruel, I can tell you. You're one mean person, Mairi!"

She spat out her words contemptuously. The hatred in her voice was tangible, and she threw in scorn and sarcasm for good measure. Feeling triumphant she cast Mairi a final dirty look before returning her gaze to the glowing embers of the dying fire.

Mairi began to shake visibly. Her hands went up to cover her face. She said, muffled, "I'm sorry. I didn't mean to...not you. But once I started it was so easy. I couldn't stop myself."

"Oh, pass me a hanky somebody! Am I supposed to feel sorry for *you?*" Donna went on. "What did we hear in class the other day? 'An ally alienated is an enemy created.' How else do you think I should feel?"

Mairi flushed vividly. The crimson line began at her neck and then rose, swift and smooth like the first wave of the tide, up past her blonde fringe. She wiped her eyes, and said, "You wouldn't understand."

"Try me!"

"You wouldn't know. My father is an alcoholic, a

secret drinker. Nobody knows, except Mum and I - at least, I think that no-one else knows. Anyway, he won't admit it, and rages at Mum and I if we get on to him."

Mairi sounded flustered and, all the time she was speaking, her eyes flickered from Donna, to the fire, and back to Donna again. She cleared her throat and continued in a rush of intensity.

"Mum doesn't say much to him, anyway. She's so couldn't-care-less. When Dad lost his job a couple of years ago - he took his anger out on her. She is a nervous wreck. She's been on Valium ever since. I...I know now that drinking and pill-popping can carry a person right out of reach of their own feelings. They don't give a toss about each other. Or me."

Donna thought back to her few visits to Mairi's house. She never thought it strange at the time that they went straight up to Mairi's bedroom. Then she remembered meeting Mr Martin, a blurred outline of a man. Now she realised that perhaps it wasn't just her faulty memory that caused that blurred outline.

"I was your friend, Mairi," Donna said hastily. "Why on earth didn't you tell me? Anyway what's that got to do with stealing? Some lame excuse!"

"Oh, Donna! How can you understand?" Mairi pleaded, casting an eye around Donna's beautiful home with its many luxuries. "You've got everything - I had nothing. We were friends and I wanted to keep up with you. I had no money - so it became an easy option. The first time I was scared, but then I got used to it. In the end, I never stopped to think about it."

"So you carried on. You got a kick out of it!"

"Uh-huh. It brightened up my dull home life, I can tell

you. See, I used to go straight to my room after dinner every evening. I hated sitting with them. Dad glued to the telly, a beer can and a beer belly. Mum chain-smoking, reading some trashy book. The place like a tip. My room was my private place. I would rearrange things. Make it nice. I can see by your face you don't understand!"

"I'm trying to!" Donna said, as her friend watched her apprehensively. "But why didn't you tell me about your problems at home?"

"You'd be shocked."

"So what?"

"And you would pity me. I couldn't cope with that. I wouldn't be the same as you, or the same as the other girls. I would be someone that people felt sorry for."

"You wanted people to look up to you. Not pity you."

"Right! 'Victims' don't have a long shelf life when it comes to popularity polls, you know that? And I would feel isolated from *normal* people."

"Okay, Mairi. I understand that bit, I think," Donna said, refusing to respond with sympathy. "But, *why* did you let me make waves about Stewart? Can you not see how much trouble it's caused between us?"

There was a change in Mairi's expression. Indefinable, like a ripple over still water, and Donna concluded that it was shame. Mairi bit her lip before answering, "Guess I was angry with him."

"Gave you the Big Heave before you ever got a date, was that it?"

"Oh, he told you then?" Mairi's voice lowered a fraction. "See, I fancied Stewart from the minute I saw him, but he gave me the cold shoulder. I knew it was wrong to blame him, but I reckoned he deserved it."

She sniffed and suddenly her tone changed. "Oh, Donna, it won't happen again! Please don't report me. I don't know what my father would do to me! I'll give you back the calculator - tomorrow. I need your help...*please*!"

"Huh - I should report you!" Donna snorted. "I won't this time but, for your sake, you'd better not steal one other thing, or else I won't be so soft next time around!"

Her voice was shrill and superior and she watched with disdain as Mairi muttered a quiet 'thank you' and quickly left. Donna's gaze once again rested on the fireplace where only ashes remained. No warmth now, just cold, grey ash, dismal and dead.

Sitting there, she realised for the first time, that her efforts at being good were not enough. Instead of the inner goodness her mother had spoken of earlier, there was a total absence of warmth and only cold, dismal feelings filled her entire being.

She thought of the smouldering hatred that had festered within her for the past few weeks, her readiness to blame Stewart before that, her dismay at the announcement of the coming baby, and now, tonight, a spectacular loss of temper.

The brush of gooseflesh along her skin had nothing to do with the dying fire, but everything to do with the realization that her inner goodness was a dying myth.

1 3
PARTING WITH RACHEL

All too soon, Christmas Eve was upon her, and Donna, eager to impress James, prepared for the big event in a business-like way. The long, luxurious soak in scented bubbles, the careful artwork on the face with blusher and eye pencil, the use of a heated brush to place curls in strategic positions, and the final touch to make sure she would be enveloped in her mother's expensive perfume.

As Donna gave the mascara wand a final flick, another pair of eyes surfaced in her mind's eye. A pair of grave, gentle eyes, looking at her as if in benediction. Rachel's eyes.

She remained lost in thought until her mother came in. "Is that a look of total concentration or total abstraction?" Mrs Macdonald asked, delighted that her daughter was embarking on a little 'safe' socialising. "Anyway, you look lovely, dear."

Donna had made a major effort to look her best. Her hair and make-up were expertly done, the black velvet dress stunning and the final touches of jewellery all in place. Donna was all set to go and make a big entrance at the dance - yet she was hesitant. It was Rachel - she had to see Rachel! Her mind was made up instantly.

"Mum, it's Rachel. I have to see her, tonight. Listen, I'll just catch the early bus for town, call in on her and still be in plenty of time for the dance."

Her mother began to protest but Donna could not be distracted. Mrs Macdonald watched her daughter run from the house, and wondered at the urgency in each step.

At the hospital, Donna was surprised to meet Stewart in the ward corridor. Her mind shot back in time and, in a flash, she was back in the school corridor, reliving the fear and sadness of that day. Why was Stewart at the hospital at this hour?

"Hi, Donna. I just..." His voice stuck in his throat. She thought the worst. "Wow! You look fantastic! Is all this for James? He's one lucky guy!"

Donna blushed and sat down, relieved that this time he hadn't bad news for her. "I feel an idiot in this get-up visiting a sick person, but," she said awkwardly, "I had to call in here first. Couldn't get Rachel out of my mind. Is she...is she all right, Stewart?"

"I've just arrived here myself really, so I don't quite know. She seemed not too bad when we saw her earlier today. I expect she's just the same."

He seemed relaxed and so Donna felt easier almost immediately.

"Well, it's Christmas Eve, so I thought I'd spend it with Rachel," he added thoughtfully.

Donna looked at him and admired his love for Rachel. He could be out doing plenty of other things, yet here he was, waiting to be with her. She couldn't quite cope with the feeling this aroused in her, and was thankful when Stewart continued to tease her.

"So, is Mrs Macdonald's only daughter actually bagging her first rabbit tonight? And taking him home for approval?"

"Oh, be fair!" Donna protested, and laughter floated into her voice. "I'm not embarking on an 'Operation James', or anything like that. You know, I almost envy some of the girls in our class. They move from crush to crush, easy as breathing. Look at Mairi."

"Thanks, but no thanks! Don't want to look at her."

"Well, you know what I mean. Her type. Butterfly. No boy ever mattering to her for himself."

"You have a way of seeing into the corners of everything, don't you, Donna?"

The hidden, friendly laughter faded abruptly when the nurse finally came out of Rachel's room. Following the nurse was Dr. Hopkins, who looked grave and concerned. As he ushered Stewart and Donna into a little side room, they realised that something was very wrong. The news was brief and to the point, although mixed with sympathy and care.

"Your aunt has had a severe heart attack, about twenty minutes ago. She is only semi-conscious and we think her time is short. All we can give her now is tender, loving care. You must prepare yourselves for what will soon happen. If you can - be with her for these last few hours. Although she cannot speak, she will be able to hear and your voices will bring her comfort."

Donna looked out through the window at the bare trees spreading mantillas of black lace across a moonlit sky. Far above arched a night sky teeming and wheeling with stars. *How* could she face Stewart? But she eventually turned away from the window.

Stewart's lips looked dry, but there was damp on his forehead, and two new sharp lines of pain gouged deep furrows between his brows. She moved closer to him and touched his shoulder in a clumsily comforting gesture. He shut his eyes momentarily, and, reaching out, closed his hand over hers.

No one spoke. When he finally looked up at her, his face was shuttered and gave no visible sign of emotion, but to Donna, his needy grasp on her hand spoke volumes. He managed to thank the doctor before they left the room.

Before going in to be with Rachel, Donna gave her mother a quick call, and was reassured that James would get the message. Hurriedly, Donna wiped off all her make-up, then met with Stewart outside Rachel's room. Looking at her, he seemed to notice the absence of high-gloss veneer. To Donna, his eyes were curiously familiar, and yet strange, charged with a look that made her feel a profound sadness.

Inside, the little room was bathed in an atmosphere of peace. A bed lamp provided a softly diffused light, and the masses of flowers gave off a delicate fragrance. The very noise of Rachel's breathing was a violation of this silence. The frail, uneven gasps ripped horribly at the stillness.

Stewart and Donna were appalled to see the change in Rachel's condition. Her face was haggard, cold and clammy, and the colour of putty. Her closed eyes were deep-sunk in hollowed sockets, her lips bloodless. Under the duvet her slight body looked pitifully still.

At first Donna was terrified as the initial awful aware-ness of an imminent death seeped like an icy pool into her consciousness. But after sitting wordlessly for some time, she began to feel old, protective and maternal.

While Stewart began to read to Rachel from the Bible, Donna moistened her lips from time to time. They each held a cold hand, empty of even the slightest response. The nurse left the room, closing the door softly behind her.

The evening stretched into night. Day staff went off, night staff came on. The human drama played out in Room 12 proceeded in silence, and peace.

"Oh, I just wish she could speak to us, Stewart!" Donna said as they left the room to allow the nurses to change Rachel's position. A nurse showed them into a little waiting room and brought them tea. Further down the corridor, off-duty nurses in uniform were singing carols, as they made their way round the wards in the time-honoured tradition.

"I think her talking times are over, Donna," Stewart said at last. A direct look, grave and gentle, accompanied his words.

"I wonder - does she still have thoughts? Or feelings? Does she know she's there?"

"We'll never know, I guess. But I like to think that God is in there somewhere, somehow, helping her." They sat in silence while the carol singing faded further and further away.

Two nurses laughed out loud in the corridor. For Donna it was hard to accept that life's small parade was still going on around them. Laughter seemed to be in bad taste at times like these, but then, she reflected, the staff had to find their own way of coping with illness and death. They had to find some kind of screen to cope.

"Christmas Eve. Funny how things work out," she said after a while. "I had worked myself into a frenzy thinking of this dance, and James, and the entrance we'd make together." She smiled ruefully.

"Sorry that you didn't make it?"

"No. Oh, no! I'm happy that I came here, and stayed. Don't know if 'happy' is the right word. Well, maybe it is. Yes, I'm happy I stayed. See, I felt the decision was made for me. No way did I want to do a Barn Dance or Highland Fling while Rachel was so ill.

"Anyway, never mind, James and I may be an item yet - who knows?"

Donna knew she was suddenly, desperately, trying to fill the silence.

"Stewart, didn't you say once that I was a spoilt brat? We spoilt brats usually get our own way, don't we?"

"I remember! The skirt-hider-behind! No worries, I'm shaping you up nicely." The smile in his eyes deepened as he went on. "Donna? Do you sometimes wish that we ..." He stiffened and got up to empty the contents of his tea-cup down the sink. "Sorry, no - I can't...you know...say stuff while Rachel..."

He was interrupted by the arrival of the night-nurse, who warned them that Rachel's condition was deteriorating.

They followed her silently into the side room. For a moment or two, they stood by Rachel's bed. In their new and total unpreparedness, they looked at someone on the edge of eternity. Then, two short exhalations of breath, and Rachel's Shadowland was over. Forever.

14
THE FUNERAL

A funeral at the end of December could have been very dismal. The day of Rachel's funeral dawned with a beauty, as if the year had stirred itself for one more golden finale. A late autumn, or a second summer.

In the early morning, mist had begun to form. From the moorland behind Rachel's house, it could be seen rolling down into the valley. Silent avalanches of vapour crept slowly towards the river which ran beside the village. By eleven o'clock, when the worship service preceding the funeral had begun, a great golden sun shone on the last remnants of mist which swirled, opalescent, near the river. It touched the rooftops with gold and shone off the distant Atlantic Ocean.

"Isn't it a lovely day," said one old woman to Donna, as they sat in Rachel's living room waiting for the service to begin.

"Um...oh yes, it is," Donna replied in a vacant, faraway voice. Her face showed a battleground of emotions. The wake that had been held on the previous evening had been hard enough, but this, the funeral - it was so very final.

"No snow yet though," the old woman continued. "Mind you, there's plenty of time yet! You know, I've seen us with the snow - even in March and April," she added, getting no more than a nod from Donna. Snow was the last thing on her mind. Donna was thankful to see the minister arriving. The old woman sat up immediately, and the service began.

It was a short and very moving service and as soon as the first few notes of the Psalm began, Donna felt tears well up in her eyes. The beautiful Gaelic singing - the waterfall music - which Rachel had so loved, wafted over Donna's whole being as she sat there. The beauty and pathos of those voices, rising and falling, rushing, then lingering, was pure and refreshing. There followed two Bible readings - in Gaelic and English.

> But I would not have you ignorant, brethren, concerning them which are asleep, that you sorrow not, even as others which have no hope...

> For if we believe that Jesus died and rose again, even so them also which sleep in Jesus will God bring with him.

The minister's voice was strong and triumphant as he concluded,

> Oh death, where is thy sting? Oh grave, where is thy victory?

Donna remembered Rachel's fearless approach to death and smiled softly to herself. As she fixed her eyes to the floor, she felt something as strong as touch, and looked up suddenly to meet Stewart's gaze. He too had a faint smile on his lips, and the communication between them spoke volumes.

What was he thinking about? Donna knew that, over the last few days he had, guided by John Campbell, seen to everything with a set face and unsmiling calm. There had been no chance to talk to him since their last night together at Rachel's bedside.

As the final prayer was concluded, Donna felt instinctively that somewhere in the middle of this Christian thing, this God thing, was the sort of life she wanted. Something curled up tight inside her was stirring up and responding to - to whatever it was. But it was just beyond the grasp of her understanding. And if she pursued it, what then? What then of that other life, the only one she had ever known?

The service over, she tried to collect her thoughts. To think of what was reality. Reality was this coffin, and never seeing Rachel again. Never - unchangeable, irrevocable.

The men stood up. Their business was just beginning, for women didn't attend the actual burial. Women for bringing life into the world, men for burying the dead, Donna thought, as she watched the men file out of the house. They were solemn but business-like, as they turned up their collars against a sudden chill wind.

The coffin, bare of wreaths, was borne outside onto a long black bier. Rachel's closest relatives formed in two files in front and Stewart held the coffin cord. The bier was then lifted, and Donna's eyes blurred as they began their slow thread down to the main road. The other men fell in file behind the coffin and the women were left behind; some to cry, some to whisper farewell, some to bustle in the kitchen to make the inevitable cup of tea.

Donna watched the procession, the slow, locked step,

the solemn organization of each man knowing his exact place in that perfect order. As the pairs of men carrying the coffin moved back, a new pair took up the front and the two men at the rear, without a backward glance, dropped out of the procession to stand, quite still and straight, at the roadside. They eventually rejoined the procession at the end.

She saw this slow, silent walk become smaller and smaller. The huge emptiness of the sky and the vast distance of the horizon made it seem smaller still. She willed for the procession not to disappear...not just yet, but finally it did and a feeling of sadness came over her like slow, heavy rain. 'Oh, Rachel, Rachel, Rachel.' And in that frame of mind, Donna passed through what was left of that day.

The first day of the New Year found Donna in church for the service. Stewart sat not far from her and she watched him for some time. He seemed lost in thought and looked so different without his usual sweatshirt-and-jeans uniform.

Outside, after the service, it seemed as if everyone clustered round him, but finally she got to him, just as he was leaving with John Campbell. "Donna, can you meet me up at the old bridge. Say four o'clock?" She nodded and wondered what he'd have to say.

Having nagged her mother into having an afternoon nap, and quickly rattled through the dishes, Donna made her way up to the old, wooden bridge. A moorhen woke at her passing. Its harsh cry ripped at the silence of the moors. The disturbed heather stirred up, as though in anger at being disturbed.

The scene she looked on as she approached Stewart

was solid and lonely. The moors stretched away to eye-limit on either hand, their heavy brown heather only seeming to come to an end at the grey mourning mountains in the far distance. Miles and miles of sky looked over them, a dark, sweeping sky, ever changing with its movements of clouds. Stewart appeared to blend into the landscape as he leaned against the bridge, dropping stones into the water. He smiled as she approached.

"Hi. How are you, Stewart?" she asked.

"Surviving, I suppose. It's hard though, now that it's all over. The house is empty - I can't even go in there any more. I'm still at John's; they're really good to me."

"This will be the hardest time, Stewart," Donna said softly. "Just trying to get used to not having her around any more, not finding her there by the fire when you come home from school. Things like that."

He nodded and dropped a few more pebbles into the burn below them. When he eventually spoke, his voice was shot with grief.

"My macho image would die an instant death if I told anyone how much I'll miss Rachel. Honestly, I never knew there were so many ways of missing a person! I felt, those last few weeks, that I did all my grieving for her. I grieved to see what that blasted illness was doing to her."

"Uh. I know." Donna stumblingly looked for the right words. "And now we'll just plain miss her. You know something else that I'll miss?"

"What's that?"

"This sounds selfish. But I'll miss being needed, being good. It was so very easy to be good to Rachel. Small things, getting her iced water, plumping up her pillows - remember how we used to struggle to move her up the bed a bit? She would laugh and say that we definitely weren't cut out to be nurses!"

They wandered into reminiscence for a long time while the low January sun slid below the horizon and the light faded from the sky. The still-flushed clouds of sunset had darkened and grown cool. Below them the sky lay still and clear, for a few moments stained a pale green. The narrow river reflected this in its luminous streams of bubbling foam.

"Anyway, Donna, I wanted to meet you up here for two reasons," Stewart said, as bent his head to look down at the river.

He fumbled around in the pocket of his leather jacket, and took out a small black box. Turning towards her, he handed it to Donna. She looked at him then slowly opened it. There lying on a bed of red velvet, was a ring - an engagement ring.

Donna's heart skipped a beat as she looked first at the ring, then at Stewart's face, then back to the ring once again. Even in that uncertain light, the gold of the ring gleamed richly. On either side of a huge ruby stone sat two diamonds. It was breathtakingly beautiful and Donna could only gasp, "Stewart! Oh Stewart! It's absolutely gorgeous!"

"It's for you, Donna," he began quietly. "She wanted you to have it. Rachel left the house and things to me, but she wanted you to have that ring. Wear it, Donna. It will always keep Rachel in your mind."

"Are you sure?" Donna said in a strange, small voice. For one blind, idiotic moment she thought that the ring was from him. She tried to camouflage her feelings while fitting the ring on to the third finger of her right hand.

91

"Positive!" Stewart answered. "Take it. It's yours."

"Maybe you'd better keep it and, one day, give it to some girl."

"Don't be daft!" In the dusky sky, the moon had risen. The pale light fell between them, slantingly, from behind Donna's left shoulder. The angled shadows it cast made it difficult for her to read Stewart's expression. They stood in awkward silence.

"Donna," Stewart said suddenly. "I've something to tell you."

15
BELIEVE IT OR NOT

Donna felt stupid at having thought what she did about the ring. Her mind was still whirling from mixed emotions, but she calmly asked, "Well, what is it?" She felt that anything which would change the subject would come as a great relief. "Come on," she added light-heartedly, "don't keep me in suspense!"

Stewart paused for a moment and then turned to face her squarely. "I've become a Christian."

"Oh."

This time the silence was electric. The early evening was so still that Donna felt she could hear her own heart beat. The sound of the stream's hurrying, scurrying water, its call and babble, its never-ending murmur, formed the background to the silence between them. In the distance she could hear the traffic on the main road.

"Is that all - 'Oh'?" Stewart finally asked.

Silence again. Two long beats of it. How could she tell him of the disappointment she felt, rising now as a hard ball in her throat? How could she voice her hope that he had been on the verge of deepening their friendship? She couldn't continue to feel that way about him now that he had become 'one of them'. Anger rose suddenly within her as she let her feelings spill over.

"I don't believe this! A Christian? Look, I believe in

God too, you know Stewart but...but if you've become one of those fanatical, 'God-squad' idiots - or whatever you like to label yourself - then I feel really sorry for you!"

The wild and whirling words were out, and couldn't be stopped.

"Stewart, don't you realise, it'll be no more fun, no good times, nothing - just suit, tie and good talk from now on. Sure, I'd like to be like Rachel, some day, but I'll wait till I'm eighty and not just eighteen! See, that way I'll get the best of both worlds."

"Donna, who says you'll be *around* at eighty? You're never too young to die."

"Oh, spare me the dramatics!" A desperate fixed grin was clamped on her face, but her mind was going at a hundred miles an hour. "Anyway, it's probably only a reaction to Rachel's death. You're over-emotional just now, lonely rootless and anchorless. Or whatever."

"You don't understand, so you try and explain it away!" Stewart protested, but then added gently, "I hardly understand it myself. I feel so different. I feel as if I'm sealed inside some kind of peace capsule. And it's cushioning me from everything, worries about the future, regrets about the past, problems of the present. The lot."

"When did all this happen?" Donna moved slightly so that she could see his face, now bathed in the mysterious light of the moon.

"I suppose I've been thinking things through, the last few weeks. You say that you want to die with a real, personal faith like Rachel had. Rachel's last few weeks made an impression on you too, isn't that right?"

Donna nodded and he continued, "But, Donna, I wanted to *live* like her, not just to die like her."

"But you never let on. You never said anything."

"No, but you know how I had to read a bit of the Bible every day to her? Well, at first I found it downright embarrassing."

"It didn't go with your macho image?"

"Right! But then, it became a painful experience. See, the Bible was so frank about the state I was in. I was far, far from God. I couldn't keep all his laws, even if I wanted to. And I hadn't wanted to. I was a million miles from what God wanted me to be. I was outside his kingdom."

"Oh, come on!" Donna interrupted. "I know you were an absolute horror when you came here, but you've improved."

He smiled. "Sure, I could compare myself favourably with some people, but - in front of God - I couldn't even lift my head."

Stewart paused momentarily and Donna shuffled uncomfortably.

He went on, "I tried changing my behaviour a bit - but the more I tried the more I realised that it wasn't my behaviour that needed changing. It was me.

"And then, I read in the Bible that not only does God accept Christ's death instead of the believer's death, he also accepts Christ's life instead of their life. Christ had no fault - so God sees the believer as having no fault. He sees them just as acceptable as his own Son."

"So now you're acceptable to God. Well done! Congratulations! Join those other superior fanatics who think like that, and just leave the rest of us in the gutter! You should care, now that you've managed to clean up your own act!"

She turned abruptly on her heel and began walking

homeward down the old sheep track. Stewart quickly caught up with her, determined to make her understand.

"Look, Donna," he said, almost explosively, "a couple of days back, I was up there at Rachel's grave. I lowered the coffin with the others and saw the finality of death in that grave. Yet as I looked, I knew that it wasn't final for Rachel; she had gone to a better place.

"Then I thought, 'Is that the end for me - just a hole in the ground? A life of eating, sleeping, working, having small ambitions, achieving them, then looking for something else. And all the time blocking out thoughts of the meaning of life and eternity with constant noise - pop music, TV - filling all the empty spaces in my life with my bike, school, girls, good times; later on maybe, family worries, business cares, holidays - anything so that I don't find time to ask - Why was I born? What am I here for? What's the meaning of life? Is it all really going to end with being put a few feet under the ground?"

Donna's heart beat lightly, and fast. His initial hatred for her she could cope with, but not this. Not this.

"I try and lead a good life," she said, blocking out thoughts of the instant death of her own inner goodness some weeks back.

"*Your good deeds are like filthy rags* - remember, that was one of the things we read to Rachel? So it doesn't make any difference how good you try to be. That alone won't bridge the gap between you and God. See, what I read showed me that sin had separated me from God - nothing I would do could bring me close to him. Only a belief that the blood of Christ could take away my sin."

"Oh, that slaughterhouse theology," Donna repeated her father's patronising phrase. "Gives me the creeps!

No thanks - not for me!" she continued firmly.

" 'No' is also a choice. 'No' is a decision too, isn't it?"

"Look, it's getting on. Got to go."

She was frightened at the storm in her heart and at the suddenness with which it came on, as well as at the strangeness of an entirely new sensation. She could not put a name to it, but she wanted to leave, fast.

Stewart made a sudden little movement almost as if he would have detained her, but he did not touch her. By this time, they had reached the bottom of Donna's croft. She went through the gate, banging it loudly behind her. But she did hear Stewart's parting words.

"Donna, don't stay an outsider from God's family. Don't stay too long out in the cold; come into the warmth."

16
A NEW YEAR BEGINS

The first two weeks of the new year flew by and Donna was caught up in the mad merry-go-round of yearly celebrations. At times Donna wished she could stop the world and get off. There were too many changes in her life. The expected baby, her shattered relationship with Mairi, and now, a new Stewart - a Stewart who could almost belong to another planet for all the contact she had with him. Donna was still confused and couldn't sort out her feelings, or deal with them at all.

In that frame of mind, she left the house to make her way to the Friday night Youth Club. It was another cold, clear, frosty night. Snow had begun to fall, small and light and floating like swan's-down. It was hardly the blizzard that they'd been warned to prepare for, she thought smugly as she began to walk the short distance down to the Club.

Out of the darkness, she saw Stewart, as he made his way to Duncan's weaving shed. Her heart missed a beat and she began to panic, but it was too late to avoid him.

"Hi, Donna," he said, "are you off to the Youth Club then?"

"Yes, I'm fed up of swotting the impact of the suffragette movement on the role of women. Here's one female who wants liberated - from studying!"

She looked at him, her eyes puckered against the falling snow. Aiming for a nonchalance she did not feel, she added teasingly, "Of course, that's not where you're going! Against your religion I suppose?"

"Not exactly. There's nothing wrong with the Youth Club." He paused, searching for the right words. "It's just that I wouldn't feel at home there any more. It would be a tinny kind of enjoyment for me - thin and empty."

"Well, I have some good times there," she retorted, "and I'll never say I didn't, no matter what happens to me!"

"Okay, okay. That *was* below the belt." He sighed, "I don't mean to sound patronising, honestly. I guess I'm not very good at explaining how I feel."

"I'm *trying* to understand, Stewart!"

"It's like this. When I went to church and then to the Youth Fellowship, someone asked me, 'How do you feel among us?' I said, 'I feel I've come home.' And that's the difference. I feel I belong with them."

She was silent and he carried on.

"You see, Christians, whatever their weaknesses, they are like members of the same family. No, not 'like' - they *are* members of the same family. The same blood has bought them. The same Spirit is in them. They are going to the same place - heaven."

"Hey, listen, don't get into a lather preaching at *me!* If I want to be preached at, I'll go to church. So check your congregation before you set your mouth in motion, right?"

"Wow! Who said, 'I'm trying to understand'?"

"A woman's privilege to change her mind. And I don't want to understand. That kind of faith is a no-go zone as far as I'm concerned."

She smiled, but there was a curious finality about her voice. "I'll need to get going now. Maybe I'll see you around."

"Wait Donna, please don't go yet. I heard that James took you to some wedding dance. How did that go?"

"Oh, it was great fun, but..."

"But?"

"He's not you."

The three little words were like pebbles striking against the silence. The silence stretched until Stewart put a finger under her chin and looked into her eyes, then he dropped his hand.

"Please, Donna. Don't."

It was hard trying to unsay it. "I shouldn't have...stupid of me. Forget it." Oh, why hadn't she been more important to him! It all hurt so much and she badly needed to tell him all about it - her hopes, her dreams. But now, it was so obvious that she couldn't say any more - what good would it do?

She walked away, but Stewart followed her.

"Don't go. Wait. Please. A couple of weeks ago, that's all I'd have wanted to hear from you. That's true! But whatever my feelings are, it wouldn't work out. We both go in different worlds now. You've got to admit that yourself."

"I know, I know." Her teeth were chattering, and not just from the cold. "You're right. It wouldn't work out. And no way would I become committed to your faith just to suit us both. No way!"

"There's no way you could, Donna. It's not like joining a club, or society - you pay the membership fee and then do whatever has to be done, attend the meetings and so on. No. It's a way of life. A completely new attitude. No one can fake that. At least, not for long."

Feathery flakes floated down in silence and Donna pulled up the knit trim hood of her jacket. She had had a tiny glimpse of a relationship that had nearly come into being. Anything less now would seem second-best.

"Don't worry, Stewart, I'm hopeless at faking - I'm not ready for an Oscar-winning performance just yet!"

She thought with bitterness, 'Even when I'm suicidal, I'm funny.' As she moved away she called back, "Let's send this conversation down into the annals of history - you know, as in, 'Forget it.' "

She was still shaking as she stood in the Youth Club coffee room. While the brightly-lit Youth Club crowd swirled round her, she laughed and chatted and tried to forget. The deafening babel of young voices was earnestly and dogmatically discussing topics ranging from women's rights to the Old Firm game between Celtic and Rangers.

"The next move must come from him," she thought. "And if it does not come, it does not come." The decision - what other decision could there be? - came on a flash of pride that steadied her wheeling thoughts. It brought her back to something near calm, and slowly she began to concentrate her attention on the current topic of conversation.

With a sinking heart, she realised that the S.S. gang - and other interested individuals - had Stewart under discussion and were giving him a very raw deal.

"Yeah, right gutless wonder; just who does he think he is, just because he's all holy and righteous all of a sudden! Just wait until some things get stolen from John Campbell's. Stewart will have to confess all!"

"Huh...we're not good enough for his holiness now. Maybe we should tell his new friends about their light-fingered wonder-boy!"

Laughter went all around the room as the malignant voices continued.

"Doesn't come down here any more but maybe that's not a bad thing; he might pinch our pin-ball machine!"

Donna listened to the ongoing hostile tirade and felt the old familiar anger come rushing to the surface.

"Shut up, all of you! *Shut up!*" The crowd turned round to face Donna. White faced and angry, she had switched off the music.

"For starters, Stewart didn't steal a thing - okay? Get that into your thick heads - not one thing! Yes, I did blame him, but I was *wrong!* It wasn't him, so give the guy a break. And if he wants to join the God-squad, that's his business! It doesn't affect any of us, does it? So why don't you all leave him alone and choose something else to talk about!"

Once the stunned onlookers got their breath back, there was an immediate flurry of fiery questions hurled at Donna.

"Who then? Who did it? Go on, we're waiting." More voice joined in. "Tell us! Maybe she doesn't want to. Was it you? Yeah - who was it, Donna, tell us!"

The clamour of questions reached a crescendo until Donna shouted, "Stop! Give me a break, will you?"

Her heart thumped in her chest with frightening loud-ness and it was with difficulty that she kept her voice from trembling.

"It wasn't me! And...and I'm not saying who it was. Surely it doesn't really matter! You don't *have* to know, do you?"

But that comment only served to increase their growing suspicion. "It was you, wasn't it? Well, you little thief, you little thief!"

Soon the chant began, as they all surrounded her in a semi-circle, all accusing, all passing judgment. As the seconds ticked by, Donna had a feeling of deadly helplessness and could only gaze stupidly at the sea of hostile faces.

The outer door banged. Someone stood, framed in the doorway, covered in thick snowflakes.

"Just leave her alone! It wasn't her! She didn't take anything and neither did Stewart."

As one body the group turned round. There stood Mairi Martin, now as white as the quickly melting snowflakes which starred her blonde hair.

She took a deep breath. "It was me."

17
THE UNEXPECTED

Mrs Macdonald re-arranged the armchair cushions to try and ease her painful back. Sighing, she closed her eyes and took a small sip of iced water.

"Mmmm, I hope this eases off before bedtime or I'll not sleep a wink tonight."

Donna, head buried in a history book, looked up and smiled re-assuringly, "I'm sure it will, mum. Oh boy, am I sick of all this studying!"

"Close your book, and tell me about Mairi's confession then. I haven't heard all the juicy details," Mrs Macdonald said. "I mean, it must have been pretty exciting down there!"

"Yeah, it was! There I was surrounded by all these morons jumping down my throat. Then, all of a sudden, there was this voice shouting above the rest. It was a real riot!"

Donna paused, then added thoughtfully, "You know mum, she was really courageous to confess everything - right there in front of all of them. I mean, she could easily have slipped away. Nobody would have missed her.

"Of course, once she owned up, well," Donna mimed a downward swoop with one hand, "down came the vultures to pick her clean! The girls were worse. I suppose they had a touch of the greenies because she had all that nice jewellery and stuff, and then to find out it had been stolen stuff all along."

"I can imagine," Mrs Macdonald said acidly. "And what do you think will happen now?"

Donna was silent for some time. "Don't really know, mum. I had a chat with her and things are a wee bit better between us. But the others? I just hope they can forgive and forget, and get on with life."

Mrs Macdonald laughed out loud. "Now, Donna, be realistic. Remember I have more experience of being a youth than you have of being an adult."

Donna rolled back her eyes in a here-we-go-again fashion as Mrs Macdonald continued.

"What about the things she stole from shops? The fact that shops are in some way impersonal - does that make it all right? A few light-fingered folk like Mairi could to- tally wipe out a shopkeeper's profit and eventually force him to close down."

"I know, I know."

"Well, do you want me to get in touch with the police? In confidence, of course."

"No!" Donna protested. "No way! Look what hap- pened the last time you got in touch with the authorities, about Stewart. It must have been awful for Rachel."

"Okay, point taken."

Donna picked up the trace of shame in her mother's voice. "Mum," she began quietly, "I had to admit I was wrong about Stewart. And Mairi had enough guts to do the right thing too and own up. But Stewart would appreciate an apology from you too, mum. You *did* give him a hard time."

Mrs Macdonald didn't reply but got up slowly from the

armchair and waddled over to the window. It was the kind of January evening that made you glad to be inside. The anticipated blizzard had finally arrived - with a vengeance, and showed no signs of abating. Mrs Macdonald shivered and pulled the curtains together again.

She turned to her daughter. There was a moment's silence while they assessed one another. Eventually Mrs Macdonald spoke.

"I suppose I was just trying to safeguard our lifestyle. I didn't want you exposed to Glasgow gang influences. And I didn't want you to feel threatened by him. Maybe it was an attempt on my part to recreate my own youth - I had been so secure when I was growing up, you see. And I wanted you to have that secure feeling. That feeling that all things are sort of fixed, that all the good things won't change."

"That's where you were wrong, Mum!" Donna was stung to protest. "You wanted me in some kind of cocoon, some cosy, untroubled world. I have to leave it sometime, don't I? In another year or so, I'll probably be away at college. In the big world out there."

Mrs Macdonald looked discomfited. She tried again. "I know time will make these things happen. There's no stopping time, is there?"

She searched her daughter's face and admitted, "I was wrong about Stewart. I painted a very black picture of him. But you weren't blameless, either, Donna! You know that."

"I know. But I've apologised to him. You haven't." She shook her head dismissively as her mother remained silent. "A quick phone-call wouldn't hurt, would it?"

She disappeared into the kitchen to make a cup of coffee, hoping her mother would do the right thing. She loitered there for five minutes, before returning to the lounge.

"You're quite right dear. I should have apologised - long ago." There was a certain relief in Mrs Macdonald's voice. "I did phone him, but Mrs Campbell answered. She said Stewart was upstairs finishing an English essay and she didn't want to disturb him. She said she'd get him to call back."

"Good for you, mum! Trust him to be studying - he'll get an 'A' in his English Higher, that's for sure."

"Oh? You never told me he was that bright."

"Mum, you're a snob," Donna doodled reflectively on the notepad she was holding. "You can't equate University material with an Easterhouse ex-gang member, can you?"

But a smile had floated into her voice as she remembered her own change of attitude to Stewart when he stopped wearing a scowl and the gold cross earring.

"You must be growing up, Donna, or whatever it is that is making you see me as...as a pretty spotted human being," Mrs Macdonald said.

The teacher's brisk authoritarianism had gone and was replaced by a tentative searching for the right words. "Not so long ago, you agreed with almost everything I said. But now, you're more detached. You see me as I am, warts and all!"

"What I *do* see is one very large, very tired lady. Mum, go to your bed!"

Mrs Macdonald was only too glad to obey. She kissed Donna and walked ungracefully to the stairs.

Donna watched her go. "Goodnight mum. Hope your back won't keep you awake."

Donna stepped outside to refill the peat bucket from the supply in the bunker beside the back door. She shivered as the wind howled and whined, the snow whirling in on her and whipping her face with white chips of ice. For once she wished their house was not so isolated from the rest of the village. The lights of the little group of houses down below at the crossroads seemed to huddle together in solidarity against the blizzard. She was glad to lock the door and rush inside, where the double-glazed windows reduced the noise of the wind to a lonely cry.

Shivering, she lay by the open fire and settled to her history books once again. An hour passed, then another. Suddenly, Donna heard a slow moaning sound - not that of the wind outside, but something much closer to herself. What was it? There it was again! Where was it coming from?

Donna sat bolt upright, her heart beating wildly. In one instant, she realised it was her mother's voice! Taking the stairs two at a time, she burst into her mother's bedroom. "Mum! Mum! What's wrong with you?"

Mrs Macdonald was kneeling over the bed with her face buried in the soft blankets. She took a deep breath and spoke with dreadful slowness. "The baby, Donna. The baby's coming."

"You're kidding! Can't be! The doctor said another three weeks. And...and Dad isn't here." Donna heard the stupid remarks and knew, in a detached way, that they came from herself.

"The baby doesn't know that, does he?"

"He?"

"Oh, for goodness sake, 'he' or 'she', then."

"Are you sure? Maybe it's a false alarm."

"Who's the expert - me or you?" Mrs Macdonald's slightly jocular tone was a strain and she abandoned it as another pain overwhelmed her. "Donna, quickly, phone the hospital; tell them to hurry."

She looked at her mother and fled from the room. Panting, she picked up the phone and dialled. "Come on! Come on!" she said impatiently whilst she waited for the connection and the dialling tone. She waited, then replaced the handset and went through the whole procedure again. "Answer, please answer!" she pleaded frantically.

For a long moment the implications of the dead silence of the phone didn't hit her. It was then that she realised that her call had not gone through. There was only a long continuous tone. What was wrong? Why was there something wrong with the phone tonight of all nights?

With terrible slowness it dawned on her - the phone was dead! The blizzard outside! She wouldn't ever get through; the line was quite, quite dead.

She ran to unlock the door. The wind jeered and mocked as she screwed up her face against the blizzard. The village could no longer be seen. Her eyes dilated as she saw that the world was one enormous white blur.

Her face changed from fear to sheer terror, colour draining away. After a long moment, she swung wildly round, panic welling up in her throat. She slammed the door shut and made her way back to the living room. She stood stock-still there, like a frightened child.

Upstairs, she heard her mother's voice again, and the

sound brought on a new rush of fear, like cold water on her stomach. Outside, the blizzard worsened and the wind howled. She stood there motionless, her eyes filled with tears.

18
A PAINFUL JOURNEY

Calming herself, she moved slowly over to the window. She'd have to go down to the village and get help - even in that weather. But how could she leave her mother alone? Yet, she realised there was no choice.

She leant against the icy glass and closed her eyes. "Please God, you know what's happening here, and I need your help right now." Then her stricken conscience caused her to add, "I know that I only talk to you when I'm needing help. I know that's not right."

Then, in the middle of prayers and tears and fear, she heard a loud bang. She grabbed the curtain and half hid behind it. Then, a voice, but this time, not her mother's voice.

Donna remained rooted to the spot. Had she heard right? The storm howled and mocked after things that fled, shrieking, through the huge white that whirled round the frightened house. It was difficult to distinguish other sounds.

"Anyone at home? It's me, Stewart, can you let me in? It's freezing out here!"

This time she was sure. She ran to unlock the rarely-used front door.

Stewart stood there, his tousled dark hair sprinkled with snow.

"Donna, are you okay?" In a gesture that almost ended even as it began, he pulled her near and touched her hair. Then he grasped both her shoulders and looked at her. "Tell me! Donna - what's wrong? Why are you like this?"

"Oh, Stewart !" A feeling of weariness, born of sheer panic, threatened to overwhelm her, but she managed to speak slowly and clearly. "It's mum, Stewart! The baby's coming and...and I tried to phone the hospital to get help. The phone's not working...and I....I don't know what to do. I just don't..." Her voice tailed off as a long, loud groan came from her mother's bedroom. "You've got to help us, Stewart! *Please!*"

"Help!" Stewart's lips opened and his tongue came out to wet them.

"Is that all you can say - 'help'? Some answer to prayer you are!"

"Right, Donna. We'll need to get cracking. You boil lots of water and I'll stoke up the fire and rip up some sheets."

For a moment Donna thought she would pass out altogether. Their eyes met and she saw his comforting smile and could not help laughing out loud at his now obvious joke. And with her laughter came a swift relief that all would be well now that Stewart was here to help.

"Seriously," he added, "you get your mum and her hospital things, and I'll get the car to the door and ready for the road." With that, he went out into the cold night.

Donna raced upstairs and helped her mother into her coat and boots, collected her hospital bags and headed for the stairs. "You'd better take a couple of blankets and pillows for me," her mother warned, "in case anything happens between here and the hospital."

Donna could not think of a suitable answer for this horrific statement. Instead she helped her mother down the stairs and propelled her towards the door.

"You won't mind Stewart seeing you like this, mum?" she mumbled.

"I couldn't care less even if he had to deliver the baby himself!" her mother retorted. "Dignity goes out the door at a time like this."

Stewart came in, took the cases and blankets, smiled awkwardly at Mrs Macdonald, and went back outside. In a moment, he was back, gently guiding Mrs Macdonald into the blinding snow and the safety of the car. She settled into the back seat, "Thank you, Stewart. Thank you for being here."

She sank back on the pillows and closed her eyes. Donna locked up, pulled her hood up against a sudden flurry of snow, and fought her way to the car. Stewart had the engine running and after a few minutes of finding out which switch did what, they were off.

The car seemed to be the only thing on the road. All the while the snow drove hard until the wipers were on full. The view out the windscreen was a white, gauzy blur. They were driving right into the blizzard. Every so often the nervous silence was shattered by increasing moments of moaning from the back seat. Each groan seemed louder and longer than the last.

"Are you all right, mum?" Donna asked each time. The reply was never more than "Mmmmmm."

"A word of advice from someone who *doesn't* know," Stewart said, not taking his eyes from the windscreen and these hypnotic snowflakes. "Seems to me your mother is in a world of her own just now. She needs all her resources to get through this. Conversation is probably only a hassle for her."

"Oh...oh yes."

Progress was now at funeral pace. In spite of this, Donna had a strange dreamlike feeling. It didn't seem real, this white world whirling around them. In the back seat, her mother trapped in her own private world of pain; in the front seat Stewart trying to keep things calm by chatting from time to time.

"You know, when I got Mrs Campbell's message, I tried phoning your mum, but of course, I couldn't get through! That's when I thought of coming up to see you at the house. Am I glad I did!

"Good job you came. I don't like to make your head swell, Stewart, but it was really brave of you coming through that blizzard."

He laughed, his eyes fixed on the road. "Sorry to burst your bubble, Donna, but I wouldn't have set foot out of the house if I had known the blizzard was that bad. Anyway, it only got really rough as I came up your drive."

"My hero," she said teasingly. And then, "I think...I believe that it was God that sent you. Even though you were actually on the way before things took a nasty turn."

"I think there's a verse somewhere that says God can answer prayers even before we ask them," he said thoughtfully. "Uh...Donna, have you been thinking any more of the life that really matters?"

She did not speak for a long time. He took his eyes off the windscreen momentarily and looked at her, then looked away again. The troubled, questioning expression didn't leave his face.

"Lots of times," she finally answered. "All the time.

That day, at the bridge, I had a wee, wee glimpse of a joy that I didn't want to believe existed - and I could hardly let it go."

"So all that smart talk was for show?"

"Or shock, I'm not sure which!"

And Stewart, as if knowing her innermost thoughts, said quietly, "It's so hard to take that final step. He'll be there for you Donna; trust him!"

19
A HOSPITAL ENTRANCE

Stewart stopped by a car which had gone off the road. "I'll just make sure everything is all right." A gust of wind whirled snow into the car when he opened the door. "Won't be a sec." With that he was gone.

The seconds ticked by and stretched into minutes - five, then ten. Donna, already tensed to screaming point, could wait no longer. She scrambled out of the car, and blinded by blizzard and panic, staggered towards the abandoned car. She tugged at the door. No one there.

'Stewart!' It was a soundless, mindless scream, but it seemed to her to fill the night, to drown the wind.

"Stewart! Where are you!?"

Suddenly, she spotted him, lying in the snow, signalling to her with an upraised arm. She managed to get to him and helped him to sit up.

"Oooh! That hurts!! I can hardly move my leg and arm; it's painful."

Struggling hard, she got him to his one good foot and between them they hobbled over to the car. By this time, Donna began to realise the implications of Stewart's injuries. From somewhere came a horrible noise, like the sound a rabbit makes in a snare. Donna realised it came from her.

"Stewart - what are we going to do now? There's no-one around to help us!!" Her voice became increasingly shrill and hysterical. "What'll we do? *Tell me!*"

"Donna! Calm down! *Please!* You'll just have to drive yourself, there's no other choice, is there?"

He stared hard at her as he spoke, to get the message across in clear terms. But the thought of having to drive was the last straw for Donna and she lashed out like a child having a tantrum.

"No! I won't do it, and...and you can't make me. *You can't!*" She sobbed uncontrollably and shook from head to foot.

Suddenly, she felt the hot sting of a hand slapping her hard in the face. His hand was wet with snow. "I'm sorry Donna, but you're absolutely hysterical and you have to stop! I didn't want to have to do that. Now *please stop!*"

When the tide of shock receded, she was quiet but for dry, hiccuping sobs. She helped Stewart into the passenger seat, the snow assaulting them in a whirlwind.

A moan from the back seat and the urgency of the tones cleared any last arguments from Donna's mind. There was no other choice. She made her way to the other side and slid into the unfamiliarity of the driver's seat, grabbing the steering wheel in utter terror.

"This must be the stuff nightmares are made of," Mrs Macdonald murmured, in between pains.

"W-what'll I do first?" Donna stammered.

"Look, let me think. No better still, let me pray." He closed his eyes. "Father, thank you that you're here, longing to be gracious to us..."

Donna did not hear the rest of the short, simple prayer. The unidentified something that had for the last few weeks been troubling her mind, like a fleck at the edge of vision, now rose to the surface. She could not find words for the realisation that now came to her. She saw it with absolute clarity, as if it were a great, penetrating light, crystal pure, yet rock solid.

He was longing to be gracious. All *she* had to do was trust and believe! *He* was longing to be gracious to her!

"Hey, c'mon!" Stewart was looking at her. "Don't go into a stiff panic on me, will you? I'm too sore to start shaking you into action!" he grinned. "Listen - I'll manage the handbrake and the gear changes, so all you have to do is keep the car on the road, put the clutch in for gear changes, and keep the brake and accelerator going with your other foot. Got it?"

She smiled vaguely, "Yeah, Stewart, that's about as clear as mud! Say it all again - please!"

He did, and third time round, after two stalls, three kangaroo jumps, plus a few back-seat moans, they were finally on their way. "Help...gosh...I can hardly see a thing!" Donna stammered.

"I know, but look on the bright side. Nobody will be mad enough to be on the road tonight. Clutch, and lift off gently. *Gently*, for Pete's sake."

"Sorry."

"Didn't mean to shout at you. All right, Mrs Macdonald? Clutch. *Clutch!*"

"You're shouting again!"

"You two sound like an old married couple," Mrs Macdonald murmured from the back seat. The remark had the desired quietening effect - but only for a moment.

"You've got that steering wheel in a death grip. The car won't fly off the face of the planet if you loosen up a bit. Relax!"

Donna obeyed and the car moved slightly to the left. "Now look what you made me do!" Donna said, pulling the wheel too far to the right. Eventually she got it right.

"Okay. Point taken. Be as tense as you like."

Despite her tight grip on the steering wheel, Donna was amazed at the deep-seated composure God was breathing into her. What peace - in the moment of crisis it was still there! 'Surely,' she thought, as her steering got worse rather than better, 'surely if it was not from God, it would have deserted me by now.'

"Why the smile? Don't - it makes me nervous," Stewart joked, rather desperately, as she manhandled the clutch once again. But, as the car ate up the miles, her quiet, almost confident manner had a settling effect on Stewart. She was a rotten driver, but they had got this far.

"Won't be long now," he said, as they saw the orange street lights of the town. The snow turned the globes of light into stars which sparkled magically in the dark.

"Wow! I've never been so glad to see the town in my life!" Donna gasped as they only just made it up the last steep hill before turning into the newly built hospital.

"*Brake*! Donna, the brakes! We don't want to drive *into* the ward, the entrance will do fine!" He gave her a cheeky grin and she sighed with relief as they skidded to a halt, stopping by the big glass doors.

She could have cried with joy...but there was no time! Mrs Macdonald could only gasp, "Oh! Tell them to hurry, Donna!"

She ran, on wobbly legs, towards the automatic doors. Snow was still falling in sharp, slanting streaks but Donna was only interested in pouncing on two idle porters. They quickly grabbed two wheelchairs and followed her to the doors. She caught hold of two nurses too and fairly soon, the two patients were whisked away to their relevant wards. Donna leant against the glass panel and breathed a sincere 'thank you Lord', knowing that she *did* see his hand in everything that had happened that night.

Suddenly, to shatter her newly found peace, a porter returned and spoke in official tones, "Can't leave your car there, sorry. You'll need to park it in the main car park over there."

She looked at him and thought he seemed some distance from her. She gave him a faint, faraway smile.

"Just do a quick three-point turn here, or reverse over; just move it!"

Donna's faint smile grew shallower, the eyes dreamier. "You shift it," she whispered, "I can't drive."

With that she went down like a felled oak in a dramatic, old-movie style faint. She was just caught by the astounded porter, who quickly carried her to a nearby side-room and left her with a nurse. Donna had been through a real experience that night and she too needed attention.

When she did come round, the nurse handed her a cup of over-sweetened tea, then left her in peace, saying she would call when they had news of her mother.

Pressing heavier on her thoughts at that time, though, was Donna's need to take that final step that she'd for so long avoided. Sitting on that hospital bed, she began to pray softly, "Father, I want to thank you that you are here with me right now - longing to be gracious to me. Lord Jesus, thank you for paying the penalty for my sins at Calvary. Take me now, as I am, and make me yours, Amen."

20
A NEW BIRTH

Donna was eager to share her news with Stewart, and slipped out of the side room to look for him. Once past the 'cat's chorus' of the Nursery, the hospital corridors she walked through were midnight-quiet. She paused at the corridor branching off to Medical.

'Oh, how many times I walked that way,' she thought, her eyes blurring over. She longed for Rachel to know what had happened to her that night and wondered if such good news was part of the joy of heaven. She carried on walking, almost glad to have experienced the poignant, stabbing awareness of that loss once again.

Stewart was being wheeled into the X-Ray Department. His face was white with exhaustion, but when he saw her, he smiled. The facial transformation was startling. Not many people can inject real pleasure into a simple 'pleased to see you' smile like that, Donna thought as Stewart greeted her.

"Hi. Donna! Heard the patter of tiny feet yet?"

"No." Donna laughed. "Imagine, after all that drama! You'd think he or she would be a wee bit more considerate, wouldn't you? I've been pacing up and down the corridors doing the expectant father bit, since Dad's not here. All I need now are the cigars!"

"What a nerve, keeping *you* waiting!" he called over

his shoulder as the radiographer began adjusting her space-age machine.

Donna liked the teasing that drifted warmly back and forth between them. She cocked her head round the door. "Any broken bones discovered yet?"

"And what exactly do you think I'm here for? A passport photograph?" he said.

The radiographer gave Donna an unfriendly look and she quickly made her exit, but not before she told Stewart which room she would be in. She would tell him all that had happened to her very soon.

Back in the Maternity Ward, Donna could not settle. The hands of her mother's little alarm clock began to creep up to one in the morning. What if something was wrong? With her mother? Or with the baby? After all, her mother wasn't young. And the baby would be premature. It was not a very good start.

She shook herself mentally. She must not unloose the hysteria that was yammering away at her mind, or allow the full force of a sudden loneliness to swamp her. Reaching out for the nearby Gideon's Bible, she sat down to read it and knew that she was not alone. She was no longer an outsider as far as God was concerned.

A knock at the door made Donna jump, but it was only Stewart.

"No broken bones," he said thankfully. "Just pulled muscles and stretched tendons," he said, displaying a bandaged leg and an arm in a sling.

"Oh Stewart, you look as if you've been through the wars! Sit down. Here, sit here."

"Don't overdo the fussing-over-patient bit. And *don't* call me Hopalong Cassidy!"

"Scouts Honour - can a non-Scout say that? How are you feeling?"

"Relieved. You see, at first they wanted me to stay in overnight. I sat beside a bed in Male Surgical, waiting for pain-killers. Well, the ward was jam-packed with Grade 1 nutcases. One old guy thought I was his son and told me to bring in the sheep. Another wheezy old fellow - he must have been at least a hundred - kept shouting for his mother. I'd hate to have seen *her*! A Spanish fisherman in another bed was roaring on top of his voice because he couldn't get anyone to understand him. Or maybe it was because he was in pain."

"And you couldn't cope?" Donna said, laughing.

"Right! Oh, I know I could be like that myself one day, and I did feel sorry for them. But I hobbled out of that ward as fast as my leg could carry me."

"Oh Stewart, you're the original hopeless case!" Donna said.

But Stewart became silent, for he had just noticed the open Bible in her lap. He looked at her questioningly, and Donna wondered if she had a voice to speak with.

She took a deep breath. "I asked Christ into my life - tonight. I...I wanted you to be the first to know, Stewart."

For a second, this remark hung in the air. His face moved through a dozen expressions, and when he finally tried to speak, he couldn't. Eventually, he spoke.

"Oh, Donna! That's just great news! I'm so happy for you - more than you'll ever know! It's funny," he continued, "I've been praying all those weeks for you. But, maybe...how can I put this? Maybe my motives weren't right. Maybe I wanted you to put your faith in Christ - to suit me. So that we could...uh, you know...go out together."

"And now?"

"I think I'm getting a tiny wee glimpse of what it must mean to God. The eternal value of your soul, I mean. An outsider brought in from the cold. It could never be simply to suit anyone else, could it?"

"Never. It's too compelling for that. Tonight, I wasn't dragged, kicking and screaming, to Christ. I ran!" They sat in silence, wanting the moment to last for ever.

The door was flung open, and the nurse came in, flushed and exuberant.

"Well?" Donna croaked, going to meet her.

"Well, your mum was really tired out, but she got on just fine and had enough strength to see her through. You have a beautiful little sister, Donna! She's completely normal, disgustingly healthy and screams like a banshee!"

Donna stared at her, then at Stewart. "A sister! A sister!" she laughed, giving Stewart a bear-hug.

"Ouch! My arm!" he said, grinning.

"Ooops, sorry, I forgot!" Donna smiled, not looking terribly sorry. "And how's mum? Is she all right?"

"She's really exhausted, as you can imagine. It's all been very traumatic for her. Give her half an hour and then come back to this room. I'll take you to see her then. You can just stay for a few minutes though, as she'll need to rest."

They both nodded understandingly. Donna added, "And...and my sister. Could we see her, even just a tiny wee glimpse?"

The nurse smiled warmly. "Of course! After all, she's *your* sister! After you've seen your mum, come along to the nursery, and we'll even let you hold her for a few minutes."

Donna beamed - her own sister! It sounded so strange - but lovely.

"A sister, gosh," Donna was still murmuring, as they made their way back from the staff canteen.

"You're a woman of original conversation, aren't you?" Stewart teased.

They smiled at each other. Their hands touched, tip to tip, then palm to palm. Then they went in to see the proud mother.

Mrs Macdonald's face, pale and exhausted, lit up when she saw them. She grimaced at the blood transfusion apparatus she was linked to.

"The vampires are going on strike - I'm doing them out of good business! And I've still four units to go."

Donna hugged her mother fiercely.

"How does it feel no longer to be a single child?" Mrs Macdonald asked.

"Great!"

"Are you sure?"

"Of course! What would you do if I said 'Awful' - put her back?"

Her mother laughed, until she noticed Stewart standing in the background.

"Oh, Stewart! Come here!" She hugged him as warmly and closely as his injuries would allow. "I am *so* sorry for all the trouble I've caused you; and I will never, ever forget what you did for me tonight. Please forgive me for...you know - everything!"

But Stewart had long forgiven her and he nodded, giving her a reassuring smile.

"That's okay, Mrs Macdonald. How...how are you? I'm really glad everything went well. You'll be thrilled with your new baby daughter! Have you had time to think of a name for the young lady yet?"

Mrs Macdonald looked wistfully from Stewart to Donna. "Yes, I have," she said quietly. "I've chosen a name that will be meaningful to us all. It's a big 'thank you' to Stewart for all he's done, but, more than that, it's to be a sweet memory of a wonderful person. I want to call her - Rachel."

Stewart smiled and turned away. Donna beamed. "That's just great, mum!"

"I couldn't have asked for a better 'thank you'," Stewart finally said. He looked thoughtfully at Donna. "Isn't it funny - I got to know Christ through the death of a Rachel; you got to know Christ through the birth of a Rachel."

"What do you mean?" Mrs Macdonald shot an uneasy glance at her daughter.

"Oh, my big mouth! Of course, you don't know..." Stewart's voice tailed off, as if he lacked the confidence to go on.

"It's okay. I was going to tell Mum anyway," Donna said.

Stewart's grave, questioning expression changed quickly into a smile. Obviously he was satisfied at what he saw in Donna's face.

"Tell me what?" Mrs Macdonald asked.

"What Stewart has just said - that I have become a Christian tonight."

Mrs Macdonald knitted her brows like someone trying to see something in a new light. "Don't be silly," she said dismissively. "You're already a Christian."

"Nobody is *born* a Christian, mum. It's something you *become*. It's like this..."

"Look, cut out the preaching-to-the-lost," Mrs Macdonald interrupted. "In fact, in the interests of family harmony, Donna, don't mention this to your Dad."

The nurse came in. "Just a couple more minutes now," she said, as she quickly set things in place and left the room. Donna bent down and kissed her mother softly, before saying goodnight and leaving the room.

Outside the side room, Donna leant her head against the corridor wall. "I'm so disappointed, Stewart. I didn't think she'd be quite so negative. I wanted so much to be her signpost to Jesus."

A hint of amusement crossed his face. "Reminds me of someone else. Someone who said, 'Oh that slaughter-house theology - it gives me the creeps!'"

"Don't remind me! I was so determined to win mum with words. I wanted to launch some kind of three-pronged attack, and all I got was a bent fork."

Stewart laughed as they walked to the nursery. He said, "Never mind, Donna. Your parents will see it, even if they don't want to hear it. They'll see the change in your life."

Donna and Stewart were soon gowned and masked and inside the Nursery. Her anticipation of which baby was *her* little sister knew no bounds. The nurse walked between the two rows of sleeping or crying babies, and gently picked up a tiny bundle of baby, all wrapped up in a pink blanket. She brought the baby over and laid her in Donna's outstretched arms. "Donna, meet Rachel. Rachel, meet Donna," the nurse said.

"Oh, isn't she beautiful," Donna whispered in awe. In the crook of her arm, she held the child. The baby seemed absurdly small and light and boneless. Donna marvelled over the fresh redness of her, the puzzled, perfect face, and the soft down of the silky fair hair. "Hello, baby Rachel, welcome to our world!"

Stewart watched as the baby waved star-fish fingers, and then he smiled as the little fingers began to curl tightly around his own big one. "Hi, baby! You are a little beauty, aren't you. Don't you let that big sister of yours boss you around - okay?

"You know," he said quietly as he turned to Donna, "that tiny baby is just like you tonight. She's just newly born, yet she's complete, and already perfect. You are a new babe in Christ tonight, yet you have all you need to live the Christian life. Walk closely with God, Donna. He'll never, never leave you."

He stroked baby Rachel's forehead with the edge of his little finger. For a quiet, slow moment Donna looked at him, savouring his words, savouring this moment. She fingered Rachel's ring and thought, "Oh, Stewart, how much I needed you to share this time with me! How much, you'll never know. Or maybe...maybe you *do* know."

She wrapped the feeling up and put it in her heart. This precious moment would linger long in the air, like voices linger in the memory. There was all the time in the world to put feelings into words.